A PLUME BOOK

WHEN SHE MAKES MORE

FARNOOSH TORABI is an award-winning personal finance journalist, speaker, and media personality. Her work and advice have been featured in the *New York Times* and the *Wall Street Journal*, and in *Entrepreneur*, *Time*, and *Money* magazines. Her television credits include the *Today* show, ABC, CNN, *LIVE with Kelly and Michael*, *The Dr. Oz Show*, and *The View*. She hosted the Webby-nominated show *Financially Fit* on Yahoo!, the number one personal finance series on the Web. She lives in Brooklyn with her husband and young son. Learn more about Farnoosh at Farnoosh.tv.

Praise for *When She Makes More*

"*When She Makes More* delivers exactly what a female breadwinner today needs: road-tested, effective, and exceptionally pragmatic advice for navigating tough financial terrain while making the move toward a stronger, healthier relationship."

—Tony Robbins, author of *MONEY Master the Game:
7 Simple Steps to Financial Freedom*

"*When She Makes More* is an inspiring, optimistic book that equips today's female breadwinners with smart solutions for overcoming the personal and professional trip wires of our new economic reality." —Barbara Corcoran, star investor on ABC's *Shark Tank*

"In *When She Makes More*, Farnoosh Torabi unmasks the challenges female breadwinners face and provides solid solutions for protecting your finances and your relationship."

—Tory Johnson, *Good Morning America* contributor
and *New York Times* #1 bestselling author of *The Shift*

"I predict Farnoosh's groundbreaking book will save more relationships than couples counseling ever could. Superbly researched, well written, engagingly fun, I couldn't put it down. Every working woman, married or single, needs to read this empowering guide! I'm so grateful I did."

—Barbara Stanny, author of *Sacred Success:*
A Course in Financial Miracles

"*When She Makes More* is a book of liberation from old ideas about women in the workforce who want to have it all. Torabi's intelligence, respect for research, and vibrant prose put the book in an elite class with the best self-help books from financial gurus and masters of psychological nonfiction."

—Amanda Steinberg, founder of DailyWorth.com

When She Makes More

The Truth About Navigating Love and Life
for a New Generation of Women

$ $ $

Farnoosh Torabi

A PLUME BOOK

PLUME
Published by the Penguin Group
Penguin Group (USA) LLC
375 Hudson Street
New York, New York 10014

USA | Canada | UK | Ireland | Australia | New Zealand | India | South Africa | China
penguin.com
A Penguin Random House Company

First published in the United States of America by Hudson Street Press, a member of
Penguin Group (USA) LLC, 2014
First Plume Printing 2015

P REGISTERED TRADEMARK—MARCA REGISTRADA

THE LIBRARY OF CONGRESS HAS CATALOGED THE HUDSON STREET PRESS EDITION AS FOLLOWS:
Torabi, Farnoosh.
  When she makes more : 10 rules for breadwinning women / Farnoosh Torabi.
    pages cm
  Includes bibliographical references.
  ISBN 978-1-59463-216-7 (hc.)
  ISBN 978-0-14-218192-8 (pbk.)
  1. Married women—Employment. 2. Income. 3. Work and family.
4. Couples—Finance, Personal. 5. Women—Finance, Personal. I. Title.
  HD6055.T67 2014
  650.1082—dc23   2014001289

Printed in the United States of America
10 9 8 7 6 5 4 3 2 1

Set in Minion Pro
Original hardcover design by Eve L. Kirch

AUTHOR'S NOTE: Names and identifying details of some interviewees have been changed
to respect the privacy of the men and women who so openly shared their personal experiences and sentiments on this complex topic.

For Tim, my best friend and better half

CONTENTS

Money and Margaritas

Girls used to grow up with so few avenues open to them that dreaming of marrying a Prince Charming who could provide for them and their children was an expression of ambition. In the last fifty years, though, something radically changed. Girls began to join the ranks of men in the workforce with equal professional ambitions as they heard things like *Stick to your strengths. Never give up.* And my personal favorite: *You can do anything you set your mind to. You can "have it all."* These mantras laid the foundation for the predicament facing many of today's working women who heeded that sage advice and are now experiencing troubled relationships with men. And they are asking: how does a female breadwinner make it all work? Money is already a bone of contention for most people; when she is the one who makes more, however, the plot thickens. Money suddenly becomes a greater source of stress, a trigger for infidelity, and a major cause of divorce.

The media have had a field day with the topic of "women on the rise" over the past few years, highlighting how wonderful it is that we're finally ascending in the workforce like never before and outearning our male counterparts in many areas of the country. But this dramatic shift is rife with complicated struggles that can threaten coupledom and even spill into our relationships with friends and family members. Everyone has an opinion. But no one has the answers. That is why I have written this book. It's the ultimate guide for having a deeply satisfying relationship while protecting your income, as well as preparing yourself financially and psychologically for all the likely obstacles that arise when you earn more than your partner. Don't get me wrong: this book isn't just for the elite women out there who are banking six-figure or more salaries and wearing Prada to work. It's designed to help any woman whose livelihood depends on her income and whose intimate relationships and/or family life is affected by that income. Although the book is geared specifically toward women who make more than their partners, this topic also lends itself to much broader conversations about money and relationships in today's world. I intend for this book also to appeal to single women in the dating world whose success may intimidate potential suitors and who may soon find themselves in a relationship where she's bringing home the filet mignon. Couples who start out on even ground and then find that she is outearning him will also find plenty of useful advice here. That happens a lot, and if you're not prepared for the shift, your relationship can hit a serious, painful snag.

I knew I was in for a wild ride the day my mother questioned me on the man I'd chosen to marry. She put it bluntly not long after I announced our engagement: *Farnoosh, I just want you to be happy and not have to struggle.* Mom knew my soon-to-be-husband, Tim, wasn't going to be wealthy in the near future. He wasn't on the road to becoming a doctor, lawyer, or investment banker, having instead chosen a career as a software engineer (with dreams of starting a business someday). I gave her credit for her honesty, but what she didn't realize then (and which would have been difficult for her to sincerely accept) was that I was on the path to earning more than he would . . . by a long shot. Moreover, she could not have fathomed that my "struggle" would be about making *too much money* in comparison. She assumed we might have trouble making ends meet if Tim didn't bring in enough income. Never did she imagine that I'd make enough money to support us both, a role reversal that would bear its own challenges.

When it came time to reorganize my monetary life as I prepared for marriage and started to think earnestly about my future as one half of a "we," I couldn't turn to the established wisdom set by the Suze Ormans and Dave Ramseys of the world (and I clearly couldn't turn to my mother). Admittedly, I couldn't even rely on some of the ideas I'd learned in my own experience as a journalist and "personal financial guru" for the likes of NBC, ABC, *Money*, and Yahoo. Why? Because when a woman makes more than her man, the game is totally different. Period.

The New Landscape

Right now, more women than men place an emphasis on career aspirations. A 2012 Pew Research Center study found that 66 percent of young women aged eighteen to thirty-four rate their career high on their list of life priorities, compared with 59 percent of young men. This reflects a huge change in women's attitudes toward working that has been brewing over the last half century but has been accelerated by the recent recession. By the end of 2012, Pew documented evidence that since 2007, the percentage of mothers who said that their ideal situation would be to work full-time rather than part-time or not at all had gone from 20 percent to 32 percent.

The percentage of top breadwinning women—young and old, married and single—has been growing exponentially for decades. The latest data show that women under the age of thirty have a higher median income than men in nearly every major city in the country. Of all married couples across all ages, 24 percent include a wife who earns more, versus a scant 6 percent in 1960. For women married to men without a college degree, that figure edges up to 25 percent of marriages. (In other words, the percentage of married couples with higher-earning wives is *four* times greater than what it was in the 1960s.) So, I know I'm not alone in my journey to a happy household when my salary outpaces my husband's paycheck. The time has come for us female breadwinners to ditch the old rules and follow a different set of principles. This is the book I needed.

In general, two distinct groups make up the majority of the breadwinning women in America. Single mothers represent one group; they are more likely to be young, less educated, and African American or Latina, and they have a median household income of $23,000. The second group encompasses the married women who make more than their husbands; they are more likely to be white, college educated, and a little older, and their median family income is $80,000. (In the upper echelons of this second group are the affluent married couples, a little over one-third of whom discuss their finances more than they do their sex life!)

Although marriages in which she makes more are still relatively rare, they are increasing in number. And surveys indicate that as a society we're a bit mixed on what we think about all this. Norms may be changing, but our belief system does not seem to be moving as fast. Twenty-eight percent of Americans surveyed by Pew agreed that it is "generally better for a marriage if the husband earns more than his wife." Apparently, newlyweds are the most open to having her earn more compared with couples who've been married longer. Perhaps this is because they haven't faced many challenges yet, or they are of a younger generation that's more likely to break with traditional gender roles. In about 30 percent of newly married couples in 2011, the wife earned more (versus 24 percent of all married couples). I found this to be true both in my own research and anecdotally, from speaking with individuals and couples.

Although in general many of us are becoming more accepting of single mothers, some of us still seem to have mixed feelings about whether or not it's a good thing for mothers—single or married—to work at all. A separate 2013 Pew survey found that about half of us say that children are better off if their mother is at home and doesn't have a job while only 8 percent of us say the same about a father. What's more, this same 2013 Pew survey found that 64 percent of Americans still agree that the growing number of children born to unmarried mothers is a "big problem" (albeit this reflects a decrease from 71 percent in 2007). But most Americans acknowledge that the increasing number of women working outside the home makes it easier for families "to earn enough to live comfortably."

Another interesting trend identified by Pew: today's single mothers are much more likely never to have been married than in the past. In 1960, the share of never-married single mothers was just 4 percent; as of 2011, it had risen to 44 percent. Never-married mothers tend to make less money than their divorced or widowed counterparts and are more likely to be a member of a racial or ethnic minority. (Such a steep rise in unwed mothers has no doubt contributed to the female breadwinner equation.)

Just as there are numerous types of women today outearning their partners—from accidental breadwinners who are just trying to make ends meet because they are recently divorced, or their partners have lost their jobs, to high-powered, career-focused female warriors who wear the high heels and sometimes the pants in the relationship—there are an untold number of ways to solve potential problems and make these complex relationships work. No matter which type of breadwinning woman you are, you'll find a variety of the solutions in this book relevant to you and your personal circumstances. I've spent the past two years researching this topic and collecting proven strategies from both professionals and laypeople who deal with this very situation on a daily basis—men included. In addition to interviewing relationship gurus and financial planners, I've spoken with psychiatrists, behavioral experts, scholars, and divorce attorneys. I've also had the privilege of teaming up with clinical psychologist Brad Klontz, an associate professor at Kansas State University, author of four books about the psychology of money, including *Mind over Money: Overcoming the Money Disorders That Threaten Our Financial Health*, and the cofounder/CEO of YourMentalWealth.com. Together we conducted a comprehensive survey of more than one thousand women nationwide (most of them breadwinners) on their experiences with the impact of money on their relationships. You'll read about the very illuminating results of the survey in chapter 1.

So even though there is no "one size fits all" in addressing the issues related to female breadwinners, there are certain ways of thinking, planning, and managing expectations that can indeed make the road a little less bumpy and a lot more loving for every gal who makes more than her man or who is otherwise financially independent.

In a record four in ten American households with children under the age of eighteen, the mother is the primary source of income for the family. That's more than five million breadwinning moms, a number that has quadrupled since 1960.

It's Complicated

For starters, managing money isn't just a matter of numbers and spreadsheets; it's emotional. We don't need a book that's just about how to handle bills, debt, and estate planning. What we need is a map of how to best manage our *relationships* when dealing with this complex and delicate dynamic—in addition to knowing how to address economic nuts and bolts. Add to that the fact that our cavewoman brains haven't evolved fast enough to deal with the new status quo and that men are also stuck with DNA programmed for hunting and providing, not gathering groceries and house-cleaning, and clearly we've got a complicated state of affairs.

I navigate this potentially hostile environment every single day, and for many reasons that extend beyond the income disparity in my own relationship: I'm a first-generation Iranian American whose culture instilled in me vintage stereotypes and expectations about marriage and money. I increasingly work with other bread-winning women from varied backgrounds who share their frustrations (and winning formulas) as they desperately search for secrets to success in balancing their fiscal and romantic lives. So as I began to think about my next book, following my latest in 2010 (*Psych Yourself Rich: Get the Mindset and Discipline You Need to Build Your Financial Life*), the questions kept mounting: When you as a woman make more, how do living expenses get paid (and how do you even broach that topic with your partner)? How do retirement accounts get funded? What if kids are in the mix, or will be some-day? How do you avoid power struggles? How can a woman help her man who makes less escape the perils of feeling emasculated, and preserve his masculinity and instinctual desire to be a pro-vider? How can a woman who feels that she's got a lot riding on her, and on her income, cope with the added pressures without feeling anger or resentment?

Once I got going with my research and conducting interviews with people who live and breathe this reality daily, I realized just how complex and multifaceted this topic is. More often than not, the struggles don't stem from the logistics of managing money. That's the easy part. It's the deep and highly nuanced psychological layers that are the most difficult to navigate in this extraterrestrial neighborhood. It's much more about the mental game and emotional forces at play than the coordination of who pays for what and how to make sense of the dollar signs.

Money is a topic that makes most everyone uncomfortable from time to time, and it's the number one reason for divorce worldwide in both traditional marriages and those where she makes more. But the stakes are even higher if she earns more, as a dramatically different topography takes shape. This is an area of money matters that we cannot ignore or hide. No wonder I got through my first heart-to-heart about money with my now husband, Tim, over strong margaritas at a bar. While our society may not be keeping pace yet with this sudden, irreversible economic trend women like us have created, with the right tools, we ourselves can. And if we want to be in happy, satisfying relationships, we *have* to—we don't have a choice.

I've had a blast conducting research for this book. Casting the practical financial lessons aside for a moment, I can't wait to share with you what I've learned from experts who know about the gender differences that drive behavior. Did you know that the male brain thinks in a different way about money from how the female brain does? And that we can unintentionally belittle a man by misrepresenting our needs and creating a huge disconnect in everyday conversations? When you learn about the driving forces of our individual sex—both men and women—it can shine a light on so many issues that make managing a traditional role reversal that much easier. I also learned that there's a lot we can glean from gay couples, who, you probably aren't surprised to read, know a thing or two about making partnership work, and that even the most "brawny, protective" men like a policeman from Boston and a former marine (both of whom you'll meet) can embrace a breadwinning wife with grace.

In writing this book, I've also spent my fair share of time refereeing heated debates at dinner parties over the topic of women making more. I've heard everything from "No man would ever want his woman to make more than he does" to "No woman would ever want to make more money than her man." But here's the thing: people with opinions like these aren't living in the modern world. And the ones who are successfully navigating a very untraditional relationship have moved far past these obsolete, sexist notions. You're going to hear from some amazing women whom I've been lucky enough to interview and draw insights from these trailblazing role models. Many of these women have remarkably fulfilling lives, such as the pension actuary whose income borders on six figures, married to a school bus driver who makes $11,000 a year, and the bank executive who makes seven times more than her blue-collar husband. Both have been happily married for more than twenty years. What are their secrets to making an untraditional family life as normal and successful as can be? How do they effectively deal with disapproving in-laws and others who pass judgment? How do they share responsibilities and obligations in light of different individual needs and resources? Meanwhile, what are all these people *feeling*—are the women proud or reluctant and resentful? Do the men feel liberated or self-conscious and humiliated? How can a couple stay tuned in to one another's emotions? I'm going to tackle all these questions and much more.

The cold reality about making a relationship work when there's an unusual income disparity is that it takes a lot more effort than relationships with no disparity or a traditional income disparity. I won't sugarcoat the truth. I've counseled and interviewed enough women to know that just as many, if not more, couples crumble under the weight of all the extra stress involved when the woman brings in more than the man. Look no further than the tabloids to see this happening among many top earners in the public eye. But you don't have to be a Hollywood starlet or business mogul banking millions to experience the strain of being more financially fit than your significant other. You also don't have to be in a bad marriage to a freeloading gold digger to find yourself frustrated beyond measure and wondering how to make your life—and your relationship—work happily. It doesn't take much of a disparity to spoil all the fun. In fact, *any* disparity will create a whole new dimension for you and your man to explore.

We're going to see how this plays out in a variety of different kinds of relationships, including ones in which the imbalance isn't just financial but also educational. Many of today's women around the world—from France and Portugal to Colombia and the United States—are matching up with men who have less schooling. This brings a whole new meaning to "opposites attract" as we examine the characteristics of a healthy relationship in which the woman is seen as "marrying down" due to the obvious discrepancy in their levels of academic achievement (e.g., the doctor who marries the carpenter with no college degree). The good news is that even when people with disparate incomes come together, they can develop a deeply loving and mutually enriching partnership that outlives many more economically traditional relationships. They also can weather all the storms that lie ahead. In some cases, a woman might find herself making more because her partner decides to go back to school. Or she might be outearning her man by just a little, but the stress of keeping up with that critical income presents problems in her relationship—especially with thoughts of having children.

It's Not About Feminism Anymore

In a hundred years or so, sociologists, demographers, and anthropologists will likely look back at our generation of women and mark the beginning of the twenty-first century as the time when we flipped the "sex pool"—the place where we find mates and settle into family units. We're using our brains to land a bright career while keeping our fingers crossed that we'll find love. But that love needn't come with an enviable paycheck and a pension plan. It doesn't even need to come with a graduate degree.

Although the phenomenon of female breadwinners is so new that "the emotional landscapes of such families are somewhat of a mystery," writes Hanna Rosin, author of *The End of Men: And the Rise of Women*, it's not a mystery for those of us already living and working in the trenches of this landscape. And I don't buy into the idea that this new economic order is mowing over men or somehow depriving them of their masculinity. Much to the contrary, it's generating fresh opportunities for both sexes to benefit from as long as they learn to appreciate and embrace all of its myriad intricacies and hidden treasures. From a general socioeconomic standpoint, men are still expected to bring home the bacon, and women still feel obligated to fry it up in the pan (even after working a full day). Men are celebrated for being good fathers, whereas being a great mother is simply assumed of us. Perhaps some of these standards have evolved a little—it's common for women to work and have kids—but not in the revolutionary, paradigm-shifting way we need to understand in order to create a healthy, successful, modern relationship.

I met my husband in a business class while studying finance at Penn State. But then we parted ways for a while, as I ventured off to earn a journalism degree from Columbia University. Several years after that, we reconnected, and the rest is history. By then I had established myself as a financial expert in the media and was beginning to enjoy the fruits of my labor. But despite my rising success, I increasingly sensed the challenge of handling a relationship in which I made more. And I also realized that a lot of my friends, colleagues, and peers were in the same position. They, too, had achieved all the goals that their parents expected of them, only to be in for a rude awakening once they became the head of the household. My mission became figuring out the secrets to living with these circumstances, creating a new rule book, and then sharing it with the world.

As women who make more, we don't need articles to tell us how the changing economic and social tides are affecting us, and society overall, because it already influences our everyday lives. We feel the pressure when we talk about our finances with our husbands and boyfriends. We know that when our mother raises her eyebrow at dinner, it's because we picked up the check instead of our significant other. We experience it when someone has the nerve to prod us about when we're getting pregnant, ask about our plans on staying home or continuing to work, or judge us for the choices we've made about parenting our children. We see how gender roles affect which chores get done and which don't (to wit: working wives, including the breadwinners, still, unfortunately, perform more housework and child care than their men, a problem I'll be exploring along with plenty of advice for ceding the domestic space and avoiding feeling overburdened). Put simply, we know that when she makes more, it permeates every facet of a relationship because when we talk about money, we're talking about our entire lives. And even though men have had to endure "breadwinning stress" for generations, it's just not the same when it comes to us women. The stress we feel as primary income generators is categorically different for a variety of reasons that I'll cover. This is why we need our own unique playbook.

When She Makes More outlines ten essential rules for the most common issues that arise when women make more, and it pairs stories from couples ranging in age from twenty to sixty, from various regions and socioeconomic situations, with expert advice from psychologists, marriage therapists, and financial experts (including myself). You'll learn how to manage your money fairly without stirring fights; how to communicate about housework, expectations, and gender roles; what to disclose (and what not) to other people about your financial situation; how to make smart decisions on child rearing, with the whole family (and the future) in mind; and, among other important lessons, how to nurture a secure, loving relationship when outdated societal forces are trying to muck it up.

A quick disclaimer: this book is not about feminism. My whole purpose here is to equip you with the information you need to think smarter about choices you make. It's to help you make *better* choices—not make the choices for you. I want to see this revolution continue; we need more women out there who take a leap of faith and endeavor to be a breadwinner. Let's keep this revolution going.

As women who were raised to be simultaneously accomplished, independent, sexy, and smart, we've always been ahead of the curve. Our adult relationships and marriages are no different. Building on the work of our mothers and grandmothers, this generation of women has to bust out of the roles society has created for us and forge our own paths. "The rise of women" documented in the media is just the beginning. We've all got a lot to lose if we don't heed this message, and a lot to gain—financially and emotionally—if we do. We will be the ones who set the tone for future generations and who may, in fact, have more say in the fate of future economies than we ever imagined.

At the end of 2012, stunning results emerged from a study by a team of researchers from the University of Chicago and the National University of Singapore, showing that women with the capacity to earn more than their husbands are more likely to quit their job entirely than women who don't have that capacity. And if they do work, many downplay their potential and avoid taking the lead. "That's bad news for the economy," observes a blogger summarizing the research at *The Economist*'s website. The writer concludes that the implications of the researchers' findings are clear: "they point towards a tricky future for the gender pay gap and for an economy that can hardly afford to waste female potential." I couldn't agree more. But I refuse to accept that the marital glass ceiling might prove the hardest to break. Indeed, the dynamics of maintaining a relationship in which the female makes more can be punishing. Marriage difficulties jump and divorce rates rise; but that doesn't mean the struggle is unwinnable. The stories and ideas in this book are proof enough that this scenario can be successfully mastered. It can foster the happiest, most rewarding partnerships. And that, my friends, is what the world needs.

When She Makes More

CHAPTER 1

Rule #1: Face the Facts

I knew I had departed from the ways of my mother the day she first mentioned that I should be concerned about my well-being if I didn't marry an established professional or at least someone whose job had the kind of cachet that squashed questions about future income. In the old days, the model of happily ever after was clear: we women were to wait for a strong, gainfully employed alpha man to sweep us off our feet; men, meanwhile, were to dream of the corner office. The expectation was for us to be the submissive wife at home to take care of our man and the kids. But, as I just described in the introduction, something unprecedented happened on the way to domestic bliss for women like me. Alongside other young girls, I was encouraged—by my parents, teachers, and society—to study hard, get a great education, establish a thriving career, and find a partner worthy of my love who loved me back (and in that order). Check. Check. Check. And check.

Once I was making plenty of money to support myself and an entire family if I so chose, I was greeted by some unforeseen obstacles. Despite my accomplishments, life still fell short of some of my culture's traditional assumptions and those that society endorsed. It all urged me to rewrite that old fairy tale. But first I had to face the facts, and this became Rule #1 in my quest to prosper in this new economic order. It's the first rule I teach other women today, including those who are not yet in my position but one day will be. The main reason is clear: when a woman makes more, life is actually quite challenging in ways no one prepared her for. The facts of the matter are, in fact, chilling.

Risks and Rewards

Although the relatively rapid advancement of women in the workforce has been hailed by many as the single greatest economic development in the last fifty years, new studies point to the drawbacks of earning more than your man: you're less likely to get married, and if you do, you're more likely to be unhappy in the marriage, to feel pressured to work less, and to get divorced. Your marriage is also vulnerable to infidelity on both sides. A 2010 Cornell University study examined eighteen- to twenty-eight-year-old married and cohabiting couples who had been together for more than a year. Men who were entirely dependent on their female partner's salary were five times more likely to cheat than men who made an equal amount of money. (Men were the least likely to cheat when she made approximately three-quarters of his salary.) As for women, the more dependent they were on their male partners, the less likely they were to engage in infidelity. My hunch is that infidelity is even more prevalent among older couples, since young married couples say they're more open to the wife earning more. My conversations with divorce attorneys have further supported this suspicion.

But the fact that a woman earns more doesn't just create tensions that can lead to marital woes or an affair. It goes much deeper than that, affecting virtually all aspects of a woman's personal and professional life—from how she interacts at work with colleagues to where she allocates her money, finds time to unwind, and even chooses a mate to begin with. The study I mentioned in the introduction (done by economists at the University of Chicago Booth School of Business and the National University of Singapore) found that traditional views of gender identity, particularly the perception that it's a man's job to make more money than the wife, are affecting whether or not we marry, whom we marry, how much we decide to work, and even whether we choose to stay married. Looking at the distribution of married couples by income of husband versus wife, the researchers noted a sharp drop-off in the number of couples in which the wife earns more than half of the household income. This suggests that couples are much less likely to commit to one another in marriage if her income exceeds his. Put simply, women's gains on the economic front may be contributing to a decline in marriages and their stability in general. (And this may be one of many reasons that the number of young married adults decreased by 30 to 50 percent across various racial and ethnic groups from 1970 to 2008. Clearly, the decision to marry later in life explains part of this overall decline in marriages, but the authors of the study reckon that the trend in the percentage of women making more than men helps account for the decline in the marriage rate by almost one-fourth in the forty years ended in 2010.)

The economists also found that wives with a better education and stronger earning potential than their husbands were less likely to work. That may sound counterintuitive, but not when you consider it in tandem with the fact that women are more likely to stay out of the workforce if there is a big risk that they will make more than their husbands. After all, if a woman senses her income level can ruin her relationship, and she can afford to work less thanks to her partner's income, then why not?

What struck me the most from the paper was the finding that couples often revert to more stereotypical gender roles if she makes more. This might help explain why women who earn more than their men take on a larger share of household work and child care. "Our analysis of the time use data suggests that gender identity considerations may lead a woman who seems threatening to her husband because she earns more than he does to engage in a larger share of home production activities, particularly household chores," the authors write. Other studies have confirmed such findings, some reporting that women who are the main breadwinners still do at least two-thirds of the housework. Such an unfair and persisting inequity has been cited as another reason for why overwhelmed wives opt out of the paid workforce if they can afford to. To examine the risk of divorce, the Chicago and Singapore economists used a survey conducted in two waves throughout the eighties and nineties to calculate the likelihood of a divorce during a five-year period. In their sample, some 12 percent of all couples were divorced during this period, but the divorce rate rose by half, to about 18 percent, for couples in which the wife earned more than the husband.

Of course, the double standard is ringing loud and clear: we want our men to be intelligent and ambitious, and men have these same preferences for us, but only to the point just before we threaten to earn more than they do. And these biases appear to affect our decisions about being in the workforce as well as the health and longevity of our marriages.

Although our pay, on average, still lags behind men's, our earnings have been rising relative to men's over the past forty years and we may finally close the gap as more and more girls outperform boys in high school and then go on in greater numbers to attend and graduate from college. In fact, a brand-new 2013 Pew study finds that Millennial women are very close to closing the gender pay gap, relative to other generations: eighteen- to thirty-two-year olds now earn 93 cents for every male dollar, compared to 71 cents across the board. We're already more likely than men to get college degrees, earning about 60 percent of bachelor's degrees. We're also getting better grades than our male peers and have even regained jobs lost during the Great Recession. Men, on the other hand, continue to struggle to bounce back. In the last decade, men, especially working-class and middle-class men, have had very different experiences in this economy from the women around them. The manufacturing sector has lost almost six million jobs, nearly a third of its total workforce, and has taken in few young workers. Meanwhile, jobs in health, education, and services have been added in about the same numbers. These job categories tend to be dominated by women. In fact, of the fifteen sectors projected to grow the fastest by 2016, including sales, teaching, and accounting, twelve are ruled mostly by women.

As of 2011, there were more married-couple families with children in which the wife was more educated than the husband than ever in the past, according to Pew Research Center. In roughly 23 percent of married couples with children, the women had more education; in 17 percent of the couples, the men had higher education. The remaining 61 percent of two-parent families involved spouses with about equal levels of education.

Today's rapidly changing social mores—thanks to the successes of women in the workforce—have made for some remarkable repercussions that would have made our great-grandmothers blush. Take, for example, a surprising phenomenon I call the "genderational gap": According to financial adviser and therapist Bari Tessler Linden, men actually do mature slower than women. "For men, the sense of urgency to discover what they are good at and be financially successful is just not there as much as it is for women," she says. In other words, it tends to take men longer than women to make the same level of income or pursue higher education. For example, women under the age of thirty have a higher median income than men in the same age group in most metropolitan areas, a fact I highlighted in the introduction. It's also true that more women than men are earning bachelors and advanced degrees. I think that Tessler Linden's use of the word "urgency" is key. My sense is that she's partly alluding to the fact that our biological clock urges us to get our lives in order faster than men, as well as the fact that we feel an urgency to live up to our feminine ideals and make society (i.e., Mom, Dad, teachers, mentors, trailblazing women before us, et al.) proud.

But we can't ignore the pressures working against this new trend, chiefly our innate biology and long-established gender roles. These two important forces have remained static, which could be why women making more creates myriad sources of friction between the sexes. And women still consider the workplace to be a "man's world."

Not that everything is easy for men whether their wives make more or not. As we'll see shortly, many men suffer from the same work-life conflict that women endure. And men face a set of unfair expectations all their own: Pew found in 2010 that 67 percent of Americans still believed it was "very important" that a man be ready to support a family before getting married, while only 33 percent believed the same about women. According to Lamar Pierce, a professor of strategy at Washington University's Olin Business School in St. Louis, many men still believe that it's important for them to make more than their wives. It's a powerful social norm that's here to stay for now. So when it's violated, it can make men feel emasculated. Pierce has further shown that it can even lead to impotence. In a study Lamar conducted with colleagues in Denmark, published in early 2013, he found that in relationships where women make slightly more than their spouses, men are about 10 percent more likely to require prescription pills to combat erectile dysfunction (ED), insomnia, and anxiety. Although it's hard to prove causation between an untraditional income disparity and a man's need for ED drugs, Lamar documented a parallel between the increase in ED medication usage and the increasing gap between the wages of the breadwinning wife and her husband. The greater the income disparity, the greater the problems with ED and reliance on drugs to remedy it. This link appears to be especially strong among couples whose wives' paycheck overtook their husband's during the marriage; men who knowingly marry high-earning females, however, are less likely to suffer significant psychological consequences from future income comparisons. Moreover, an unmarried man living with a woman who outearns him is also less likely to suffer from this ego-deflating effect, highlighting the fact that "the social construct of marriage plays a critical role in how men view wage comparison."

I should also point out that we women aren't immune to the health effects of shouldering our own weight and living with this dynamic. Betsey Stevenson and Justin Wolfers, economists and professors of public policy at the University of Michigan, have found that we're not as happy today as in the past even though we have a lot more options now in life than ever before. And we are exceptionally vulnerable to more stress-related health issues such as heart attacks and strokes if we don't learn how to manage and cope with the added stress. This is very true for women who have a hard time with the responsibility of it all, particularly if they became breadwinners by default following a spouse's layoff. Emotions can range from fear and anxiety to anger and full-blown resentment. As one overwhelmed, burned-out breadwinner whose husband lost his job put it, "It wasn't the agreement we made when we married."

Another study, published in the *American Sociological Review* in 2013, found that married men who do traditional male chores such as mowing the lawn, paying the bills, and changing the oil in the car have more sex than husbands who spend their time cooking, cleaning, and shopping ("women's work"). Other studies have shown this to be true as well, reflecting deep-seated views we maintain about which behaviors are more masculine or, conversely, feminine. And this influences whether we identify certain acts as being sexy or recognize a situation as a sexual one. But there's a flipside to this coin, for we also know that men who refuse to do housework, including both traditionally male and female tasks, could trigger conflict in their marriage and lower their wives' marital satisfaction. Plenty of research, some of which I've already highlighted, has found that our marital satisfaction is linked to our spouse's participation in the household (see Rule #6).

The results from the survey I conducted with psychologist Brad Klontz while writing this book dovetail all this research. Of the 1,033 women who filled out the questionnaire, which asked questions on topics ranging from marital satisfaction to the logistics of how responsibilities get shared, those who make more than their partners (as compared to women who make less) reported less relationship satisfaction in general and less satisfaction with how chores are divided up. Moreover, the survey found that breadwinning women feel more embarrassment regarding how much they make compared to their spouse. (In fact a large percentage of top-earning women admit to wishing they made less so their partners didn't feel so bad.) They are also not as happy about their preparation for having kids and managing family life as women who don't outearn their partner (for a full breakdown of the survey results, go to www.whenshemakesmore.com).

But we don't need scientists, researchers, surveys, statisticians, and experts on gender and culture to tell us that men losing their traditional role of breadwinner can have psychological and sexual costs. We know from experience alone that when we earn sizable paychecks, such a dramatic shift can lead to guilt, shame, and questions of identity for both sexes.

"Am I Better Off Without You?"

To get a glimpse of just how tragic the marriage of a breadwinning woman can be, look no further than the experiences of Carmen and Michelle. These women lead totally separate lives on opposite sides of the country, but they share a deep personal connection without even knowing one another. They look at their husbands and think the same exact thing: *What do I need you for?* When these women uttered the identical statement in separate interviews with me, I immediately wondered how long each had been feeling so disenchanted by her relationship, for how could someone stay in a marriage while harboring such ugly thoughts?

Carmen was already contemplating divorce by the time I sat down with her to talk about her experience, whereas Michelle's mind hadn't gone there yet. It turns out that such thoughts have their own primal roots. According to relationship expert Alison Armstrong, the designer of the widely acclaimed Celebrating Men, Satisfying Women workshop, "When a woman starts making more money than her husband, the cavewoman within starts to think, 'Am I better off with or without him?' It's an unconscious thing. And it's lethal."

Indeed, it may prove lethal for these women's marriages—not to mention the dozens of other women I've spoken with who think along the same lines. Carmen's story in particular epitomizes what can go terribly wrong in an unbalanced relationship in which the woman never expected to become the sole breadwinner. Carmen's husband used to make more, but then certain circumstances caused a total flip, which I reckon is the hardest way for couples to deal with a breadwinning wife. Now her marriage of more than thirteen years is, for all intents and purposes, over. She has no respect left for her husband, whom she says acts like a slug, and he totally resents her for nagging him to go back to work.

Carmen grew up poor in Puerto Rico and came to America full of drive and self-motivation, having worked since she was twelve. Today, however, as a forty-something mother of preteen twins (plus a grown child from a previous marriage), she cannot seem to motivate her husband to work; he makes no money by choice as she toils in a small business she started with her own savings "out of necessity." Upon losing her job as a sports reporter, she had hoped that her husband, David, would step up to the plate. But he didn't. He'd been running a small business with his parents, but after they sold out, he found himself out of a job—and, at least in his view, overqualified and overeducated to find another that paid well. He wasn't willing to take just any job, even at Carmen's pleas to help keep the family afloat financially. That's when Carmen went into survival mode, opening a cozy diner in her New England suburb while also moonlighting as an actress. In her words, "I was like, 'Do something!' It's like drowning and having someone stand there watching you go down. From there, [my marriage] went from zero to sixty in the other direction."

The day I met up with Carmen in her restaurant to see her in action and finish my interview, she hid her exhaustion well, for she'd been up since five a.m. and at work since seven a.m., and would go on to close up shop at two p.m. to run errands and renegotiate the lease terms of her restaurant. Later, she'd go home to prepare dinner for her family and whoever happened to have dropped by that day. I got exhausted just listening to "a day in the life" of this fierce woman. On Tuesdays and Thursdays she tapes commercials for a local discount furniture chain that pays her a generous fee on retainer. On other days she auditions for bit parts in major motion pictures. During the week of my visit, she'd already auditioned for roles in two different movies, commuting a couple hours away to Boston while someone covered for her at work.

When I asked about the early days of her relationship with David and what had originally attracted her to him, she was candid and effusive with me, like a close girlfriend. She shared the high hopes she had early on in the relationship, which eventually turned into serious grievances. Although she briefly praised him for being a loving, protective father, his lack of motivation to financially support the family—even just a little—eclipsed most of the good things that David "provided," which at this point was just the daily after-school care of their twins. "I thought he was an independent businessman and an ambitious go-getter—all the things that he had portrayed initially," she related to me. "Because I've always been in relationships where I didn't need to be taken care of, it made me wonder, 'My goodness, it must be me; I must be putting out this aura that I can take care of myself.' Looking back, I see now that his ambitions were a façade. I overestimated his work ethic. When I met him he had his own business, but once he started to experience failure, he didn't rise to the occasion." At one point Carmen had to pawn her diamond engagement ring to pay the mortgage.

She and David constantly argue about money and the opportunities that he repeatedly turns down, including a recent job offer for six figures with a start-up company that he flatly refused since it reminded him of his own failures as an entrepreneur. While Carmen frets that she has to use all of her profits to break even on her overhead and living expenses rather than use them to grow the business, David defends his behavior with statements like: "What am I supposed to do? You expect me to take a job paying $10 an hour?" His poor track record in business also made him not want to have anything to do with the diner initially, but now that it's showing strong signs of success he's expressing interest in becoming a partner. Carmen is very protective, however, and doesn't want him to piggyback on her achievements. And while she concedes that he contributes to the family by being the main caregiver of their children, it's beside the point. From Carmen's perspective, the family would be much better off if he worked and they figured out other means of child care. It doesn't help that their twins are attuned to the tension as they witness the squabbles and watch their mother drag herself home every day dead tired. On more than one occasion, their son has plainly told David, "You know, Dad, you gotta get a job."

A logical question: what keeps Carmen in the marriage? Well, it's not the sex. She vehemently told me that her sex life is dead. She can't even think about intimacy and says that she's "literally gone asexual." Carmen is semi-plotting her exit, but two things have caused her to press pause over and over again. For one, she's waiting for David's health to improve since he was treated for a heart condition. But perhaps more influential to her final decision, and which any mom would think about, is the worry about how a divorce will affect the kids. This, more than anything else, has caused Carmen to be conflicted about when she'll walk away despite knowing in her gut that "staying is no longer viable."

Michelle's situation echoes some of Carmen's experience and resulting frustrations. But for Michelle, a working mother in the Southwest, it wasn't an unanticipated role reversal that caused trouble. Her husband worked up until they had children, at which point they decided—like many couples do—that it would be more economical for one parent to stay home and be the primary caretaker. In that case, it was him. But the arrangement backfired. And now Michelle has forced him back into the workforce not only because she felt he'd lost a sense of accountability to the family but also so she could take on a much less stressful and more flexible job as chief marketing officer for a small technology company.

After years of burning the candle at both ends as a business executive at a company that kept her juggling an impossible work schedule, Michelle came close to having a veritable breakdown on the drive home one day. The frightening heart palpitations and fears that she'd never be able to keep going at such a frenetic pace compelled her to call it quits, take a two-week vacation alone, and push her husband out the door and back to work. "The day I quit my old job was the happiest day that I felt since I gave birth to my kids. I suddenly had this blank slate in front of me and could do anything I wanted."

When Michelle and her husband, Ben, first got together more than seventeen years ago, he was making more than she was. But the tides changed over time as Michelle climbed the corporate ladder and began making tens of thousands more than Ben, a Web engineer. The economics of it all encouraged Ben to scale back his work once their first baby was born. The shift in roles worked at first, especially once their second child came into the picture a couple of years later. But eventually Michelle felt like her life was becoming unmoored. She had the job with the "golden handcuffs"—a high-powered career that came with a big paycheck but at a significant cost to quality of life . . . and time with the family. Meanwhile, Ben was enjoying his relatively stress-free life (complete with hired babysitter, housekeeper, and gardener), getting used to not having to answer to a boss or be accountable to anyone but his immediate family.

I sensed from talking with Michelle that at the center of her relationship problems is a strong resentment toward Ben's lack of ambition and overall complacency—the same feeling that Carmen has toward her lackadaisical husband. The longer Ben remained a stay-at-home dad, the less motivated he became. And even though both of these women credit their spouses for assuming the larger share of the child care, the lack of drive or passion for something beyond the home front galled them. Michelle described her level of anxiety to me perfectly: "Women stress more than men to begin with, and [the unfairness of that alone] causes resentment. I would come home with deadlines to meet and presentations to prepare for the next day and then I find out my child has a 104 degree fever . . . and I look at my husband and go, 'How much stress do *you* have?' I think there's just no accountability. As a working woman there's a lot of accountability. But men at home seem to get away without having that accountability factor, which brews the resentment. I think, why am I carrying all the stuff on my shoulders? He calls me up at work and goes, 'What do you want to do for dinner?' And I'm, like, 'I didn't even have lunch yet, but I'm glad you're thinking and worried about dinner.'"

She added: "It's not as exciting when he takes money out of my bank account and says, 'Hey, I'll take you to Paris.' In the last ten years I've reminded him many times, 'You don't have to be making a gazillion dollars; you can say, 'Last year I put away my entire $50,000 salary for our kids' education.' That is the piece that I don't see. I'm not disappointed, angry, or upset. I'm disenchanted. . . . It's not enough to just love each other. We have to do laundry, clean the windows."

Now that Michelle's husband has returned to working outside the home, he's rebelling in subtle ways that further irk and exasperate her. Although she doesn't think twice about taking care of all the little things that need to get done, he uses work as the excuse now to avoid helping out. "My single-tasker husband will say he needs to be at work early and stay late so he can't make the kids' lunches or get them off to school. All of a sudden what was supposed to have been a positive contribution to the family became five more jobs for me to do during the day. This isn't working for me now." As we'll see later in the book, just because men are more committed to one result at a time (i.e., in Armstrong's words, they are "single focused," taking on one thing at a time), this doesn't mean you can't speak to them in ways that encourage more participation in household chores, especially when you're taking on more of the income-generating responsibilities.

Michelle's remarks bring up a lot of good points that we're going to address throughout the book. Although her situation and Carmen's are extreme—they are both with men who either won't work or resent working—their experiences bring up a lot of issues that even women married to hardworking men who earn less can encounter just the same. As women, we are indeed more apt to take on more at once, worry more, blur the boundaries more between our work and home lives, and attempt, however futilely, to fulfill that "do everything" desire that remains buried deep within our subconscious. This can be especially true when it comes to finding time to parent and generate most of the income at the same time. In Michelle's case, she has gone on to found her own consulting business while her husband brings home a steady paycheck, and she continues to orchestrate the lion's share of the day-to-day logistics of coordinating her kids' lives. She works out the play dates, manages the nanny, stays up late at night figuring out her kids' after-school activities, plans summer camp, deals with doctors' appointments, and spends an enormous amount of energy nurturing her children because of the fact that she works so much and harbors some guilt as a result. In her words, "If you want children and you're going to continue being that successful breadwinner, somebody still has to get up and take care of the kids in the morning."

So what happens when the men we love don't contribute their fair share or live up to our expectations, be they financial, household, or otherwise? What happens when the problems aren't even about money per se, but instead spring from much more complicated matters of the heart—emotions, ego, drive, sense of responsibility, respect, and integrity? We can end up like Carmen and Michelle: hopelessly disappointed in our relationships and brewing strong feelings of resentment that can be hard to suppress, let alone extinguish. And if there's another similarity between Carmen and Michelle that reflects another big issue at play rarely discussed openly, it's this: the downside of a single-income family from a psychological perspective.

While many young families feel they have no choice but to designate one parent as the full-time caretaker to make ends meet, having a stay-at-home parent can be risky not just from a long-term financial standpoint but also from the fact that it can create a gaping hole between two otherwise compatible individuals. No doubt Michelle and Carmen are very much detached emotionally from their husbands. When both spouses work at least some amount outside the home, on the other hand, they have more common experiences, have more to talk about, and can better relate to each other's problems and emotions. After all, how many arguments in single-income families start when the (tired) income generator arrives home at night to a (tired) spouse who isn't connected to work pressures? By the same token, the stay-at-home spouse feels underappreciated for all the household chores that he or she got done that day. Both are looking for a break now in the evening, but asking for help from each other can spark conflict. (According to Sharon Meers and Joanna Strober, authors of *Getting to 50/50*, marriages in which there is a sole breadwinner break up at a rate 14 percent above average, the highest of any income split. They report that this is due to the fact that such marriages are more likely to struggle financially. That sole provider is more stressed out and the homemaker is also "probably overstressed and frustrated at being restricted to a single role.")

Today Michelle is not nearly as close to threatening divorce as Carmen, but she's contemplating a postnuptial agreement, a tool we'll be exploring in chapter 4. She wants to protect her assets in the event that she and her husband do go their separate ways. In her mind, "Why should I continue supporting him financially if we break up?" Michelle's experience also brings to light other strategies that any hardworking mother would do well to consider, such as the importance of investing in good child care the first few years of a young child's life as opposed to later on. She asserts: "You can afford to be absent during the day when your baby is nine months old, but not when he's nine years old." That's when kids really become much more self-aware and begin to learn about themselves, relationships, and how to deal with conflict. Michelle spent a lot on child care until her kids were ready for school, but it was money well spent (and yes, this was in addition to the care that her husband provided). By then, thanks to never reducing her work hours or workload during those early years, she had earned the flexibility and seniority to say no to certain projects and schedules that interfered with quality time with her kids. Today she can pick her kids up from school at three p.m.—and says that those fifteen minutes in the car with her eleven-year-old son, especially when he's had a bad day, are "priceless."

Mind you, the strategies in this book are far from mom-centric. I'm not addressing just the mothers out there wrestling with "work-life balance" when they are the family's primary income generator. I'm also not speaking just to families with slacker husbands or stay-at-home dads. Although I won't downplay the truth about children being a total game changer, especially in households where the mother makes more, the stories and ideas I present reflect the entire landscape in which women of all ages and lifestyles increasingly find themselves. Michelle and Carmen represent a small piece of the picture today, which encompasses a multitude of different scenarios across a wide spectrum of possibilities. Their situations may be at one extreme, but plenty of other conditions that make life extra grueling can exist in a relationship where she makes more. We'll meet a childless TV reporter later on who makes twice what her playwright husband earns and feels a lot of stress in one particular department: career. She doesn't know how she'll maintain her career to keep everything afloat and even contemplate kids in the future.

If there's one thing I've learned from all the people I've talked to over the years and interviewed during the research phase of this book, it's that a vast array of factors come into play to make each person's circumstances uniquely different. These factors are cultural, financial, age and generation related, and even philosophical. A twenty-something financially independent woman seriously dating a man who makes less will think, act, and have a different set of goals and expectations than a fifty-something newlywed who has children from a previous marriage and whose new husband will never outearn her. Nevertheless, both women can have similar challenges as they navigate their relationships under the force of this new dynamic.

New Reality, Old DNA

For most of us women today, our fathers and grandfathers derived a large part of their sense of identity from their ability to provide and protect while our mothers and grandmothers shaped their identity from their family and domestic duties. But we're no longer living up to these classic standards of identity. Our attitudes might have matured a little (i.e., many of us don't want or expect to be "kept" anymore, and men are generally happier to help out around the house and with child care), but our personal lives are still heavily defined by the experiences with which we grew up. This may be why many women in the primary breadwinning position are not entirely comfortable, but they also feel that being a full-time housewife is dialing back their ambitions. And while their men may take pleasure in their success, the women can be secretly frustrated and disrespectful if their partner doesn't match their hunger and earning power. No joke: according to one survey, almost three-quarters of women admit that they would prefer divorce and raising their kids alone if their spouse wanted them to be a housewife or work just part-time.

Another way to understand all the latest statistics and accompanying clashes and conflicts between men and women is to consider that our culture—our economic and public lives—has changed faster than our social and emotional lives have. And our old-fashioned brains haven't caught up to any of this; our DNA doesn't want to progress, but our conscious minds don't want to turn around, either. As Brad Klontz clarifies, while we might be cool with a female breadwinner on a cognitive level, unconsciously our brain still expects a man in that role. This dissonance affects attraction, since both men and women use the unconscious brain to determine whether or not someone of the opposite sex is good-looking, and what assets that person would bring to a relationship, before fine-tuning it with their thinking, conscious brain. In that situation, a woman's brain would initially signal that a man who doesn't make as much money as she does would be less appealing, and the man's brain would signal that a woman who makes more could be threatening because he wouldn't have his role as alpha provider.

And as women we somehow feel responsible for taking on more

of the housework even if we have a full-time job and make more money. This is probably because there's still an expectation there to fulfill. (By the way, Salary.com lists the job of being a housewife as being worth $135,000 annually.) As we'll see later in the book, men differ in terms of how they approach doing the housework (i.e., there's a biological reason he feels the need to make a list of what needs to be done before actually tackling it). What's more, our innate biochemistry clashes with flexible—and sometimes totally reversed—traditional gender roles. As therapist Bari Tessler Linden admits, "Men still do have a need for being providers, and a lot of women still want to be rescued or taken care of."

Suffice it to say, anyone who claims men and women are equal in society is as delusional as those who think we live in a postracial world. It's nice to pretend we're more evolved, but it's time to get real and figure out how our caveman/cavewoman parts can catch up. The feminists of the 1960s could not have predicted all this confusion, much less prepared the twenty-first-century breadwinning woman for it. We've arrived at the future our feminist leaders campaigned for decades ago, but many of us are not fully equipped to deal with the inevitable, often painful adjustments that come with the shift. It's nice to finally be "the richer sex"—a term coined by Liza Mundy in her seminal book—but it's not easy to negotiate this new frontier that's loaded with pitfalls, land mines, and unfamiliar territory. Our egos and sense of identity are sitting on the edge of a cliff.

Know Your Trade-offs

Of all the lessons in this book, perhaps the most important one of all is this: all decisions have trade-offs. You're not always adding quality to your life with any given decision. Unfortunately, as women we tend to make decisions with shortsighted lenses. And that can be dangerous.

I recently came across an article in the *Harvard Business Review* that talked about how smart decisions get made in business. As the article pointed out, one thing we may forget to consider is any changes in trade-offs over time as circumstances and economics change. In other words, as the facts of the matter change, we need to stay attuned to that evolution and adjust accordingly. Solutions to problems aren't static; they are moving targets.

I find this concept to be extraordinarily relevant to the task of "facing the facts" and navigating the trade-offs in our complex personal lives. Fifteen years ago the trade-offs we had to consider in making decisions were very different from what they are today. Back then the economy, for example, was strong enough to support a single-income family, whereas that's not necessarily the case nowadays for most people. So if you're making the decision to have a stay-at-home parent in today's world, it's not the same trade-off as before because the stakes are higher. The lesson here is not to rely on antiquated trade-offs. You have to reevaluate the trade-offs today before making decisions. You have to continually face the updated facts and leverage them when you consider your options and rewrite your fairy tale.

And to some degree, the process of rewriting the fairy tale (Rule #2) is also an endeavor that's constantly in motion.

RULE #1 RECAP

- When you make more than your man, the odds are stacked against you in many ways: you're less likely to get married; and if you do, you're more likely to be unhappy in the marriage, to feel pressured to work less, and to get divorced. You're also more likely to revert to more stereotypical gender roles at home, resulting in you doing the lion's share of the housework and child care.

◆ When men lose their traditional role of breadwinner, both men and women suffer psychological and even sexual costs (e.g., impotence, lack of intimacy, sense of attraction). The shift can lead to feelings of guilt and shame and questions of identity for both sexes since our old-fashioned brains and DNA haven't evolved fast enough and caught up to modern culture.

◆ The most dangerous feeling we can have toward our partner is resentment and wondering if we're better off without him.

◆ The most basic rule of all in learning to live with this new reality is to continually face the changing facts and know your trade-offs as you aim to make good decisions.

CHAPTER 2

Rule #2: Rewrite the Fairy Tale

Many women insist that their high salaries are not a problem. Some will even go so far as to suggest that conversations about income imbalances whereby women make more are categorically ridiculous and sexist—that entertaining the problems that arise under such circumstances is downright archaic and insulting. (Indeed, I've had enough casual conversations with people to know that this topic can make many of them unabashedly incensed and irrationally opinionated. One female editor at a top publishing house read my proposal for this book and said she and her coworkers "just didn't see this as a problem" and that I was "hopelessly naïve.") But then why are the statistics about infidelity and divorce among female breadwinners so extraordinarily high? And why do some of us feel as if we're barely breathing as we try to cope with the imbalance, which also causes a breach of power that we cannot ignore? In my view, some of us are living with our heads in the sand, for we cannot brush off the numbers that reflect the potential peril of our relationships. If we're going to achieve a happy ending, we need to stop living in denial and abide by Rule #2—rewrite the fairy tale—once we've faced the facts.

The reality is that more than a half century after feminism came to the fore, many of us, dare I suggest, are still grappling with who we are, who we should be, and what we can do. We're constantly searching for the right rules to live by that will get us to where we want to be (once we figure that out). But at the same time we still live with ingrained belief systems and traditional expectations of ourselves that can compete with our modern needs, goals, desires, and circumstances. And none of us ever wants to feel stuck— another hitch for this new generation of female breadwinners. If we're making a living for not just ourselves but others (a husband and maybe children), then there is often no longer even a hypothetical choice to cut back or stop working for personal or family reasons. And if you do plan to scale back your work temporarily to accommodate children, for instance, you need a strategy. You shouldn't just opt out entirely, downsize, and let your man take over.

Happy Endings Buck Tradition (for the Most Part)

As a newlywed without children yet, I highly value conversations with people like Hannah, who has the benefit of hindsight in which to couch her ideas. An attractive suburban mother of two teenagers and wife to a police officer for the past twenty-two years, Hannah is also a top executive at a financial institution, commuting an hour and twenty minutes each morning and night and working twelve- to thirteen-hour days in an office dominated by men. To say she has broken a few rules along her climb up the ladder is an understatement.

Hannah's happy life is a hymn to this new economic order. It may not be in her DNA to live with the social and practical consequences of earning so much more than her husband, but she's definitely learned to accept and succeed at her untraditional position. Granted, she still has her own moments (during one interview, she said she had semi-joked with her husband that she's "just a money tree"), but she and her husband have hit a rhythm in their relationship that works. They met in high school, started dating in college, and got married shortly thereafter. "Right from day one," Hannah explained, "it was clear I was going to be the main breadwinner and he was going to support my career, even if that meant relocating and changing jobs so I could continue to climb the corporate ladder." But Ted did much more than pack up and move with Hannah as her career took off. He made sure that his shifts worked with being able to share child care duties and cover for Hannah's long hours.

For Hannah, being the main breadwinner and in charge of the family's financial planning, including retirement funds, estate planning, and college savings for their two children, earns her the say-so in how the couple gets to spend on needs and major wants. She's got the financial chops to do that and her husband trusts her to make the appropriate choices for their family. They understand that their family's economic security hinges largely on her income, and she must keep that paycheck coming. They also value Hannah's financial background, making her the preferred person to handle the money. Fulfilling her traditional role of caring for others in this case means paying for the majority of the living expenses while Ted's paycheck goes toward the small expenses. It also means not cooking, cleaning, or picking up the kids at three p.m. every day and supervising homework.

And while Ted doesn't necessarily clean the house or do the dishes, he does a ton of handy, man-friendly chores to keep their

home together. Speaking of manliness, we can't disregard the fact
that he's a police officer, a job that carries a great deal of honor,
helping to make up for (in a psychological sense) his lower income
level; he's not stripped of his masculinity the way other men earning less can be if they are performing jobs traditionally seen as
"woman's work." And even though the other cops at times poke fun
at him for being a "kept man," Hannah says he wouldn't trade in his
life. He likes the perks too much—his motorcycles, first-class air-
fare, five-star hotels, and never having to worry about money not
coming out of the ATM. "I'm very supportive of what he wants. I
want him to enjoy his life and have things special to look forward
to," she says. Despite saying "no, you have to wait" from time to
time when he wants to buy a big-ticket item, husband Ted has
pretty much free rein with the joint debit card for everyday expenses. If he wants to buy a lawn mower that costs $500, however,
he'll need to discuss that with Hannah first. She doesn't see the fact
that she earns more as a way of wielding the power in the relationship. In fact, Hannah will be the first to say it's not about power; it's
about practicality and who knows best to make good decisions for
the entire family.

From my interview with her, I have a feeling Hannah gives
Ted a lot of attention and freedom in many ways, which cares for
his ego; he knows he makes life easier for her and that she respects
him. And he appreciates her immensely. Seated with them at a
dinner party during the holidays, I was able to see firsthand just
how much he truly adores and respects her. The romance is still
alive and subtle gestures like opening doors and helping her put
on her winter coat make it seem like he does take care of her—in
different ways.

Hannah is quick to point out the importance of honoring and
respecting her husband no matter what. "I remind myself that he's
the one who is going to be there once the kids are grown up and

gone, and the best thing we can do for them is to stay together and stay happy. If it comes down to a disagreement between him and the kids, I will typically back him or at least pull him aside to discuss the matter." Such an attitude illustrates Hannah's lesson on the value of communication. It's the linchpin in her marriage's success, for she and her husband constantly communicate openly about their individual needs and those of the entire family.

When I asked Hannah about the one thing she'd do differently (if she could) before committing to her blue-collar husband in marriage and being the principal earner in the family, she didn't have to think long about the answer: "I would have made him live on his own for a while, or been a lot clearer about what I needed early on in the marriage. He had absolutely *no* understanding of what it takes to run a household. He had lived at home before marrying me."

Despite this minor gripe, I see Hannah as a success story— someone who has truly found a way to "have it all" on her own terms. And she's come a long way from those early uncertain days of being courted by someone who knew that the dynamics of their future life together would be different from the norm. They've managed to work together as a team all the way through being married, having kids, and shifting careers. It's a testament to the possibility of making such untraditional unions work no matter the odds.

Finding Your Stride Despite "Greedy Institutions"

In 2012, when Princeton professor Anne-Marie Slaughter penned her article "Why Women Still Can't Have It All" for *The Atlantic*, the ink was barely dry when women from all over voiced their ideas, some in agreement with Slaughter's argument that we can't have it all (at the same time) due to clear deficits in our social structures and corporate culture, while others called her complaints "self-pitying drivel." And then we have the Marissa Mayers and Sheryl Sandbergs of the world, the superwomen who seem to defy all the odds and challenges. Mayer is the CEO of Yahoo, who returned to her relatively new job just two weeks after giving birth to her first child in 2012; Sandberg, a wife, mother of two, and one of the country's most successful female executives, gave a now-famous commencement address at Barnard in 2011 that spawned her bestselling book, *Lean In*, in which she urges women to pursue their careers aggressively ("put your foot on that gas pedal and keep it there") and not be distracted by worries about how to balance work and family, especially before there's even a man in the picture. Rightfully so, Sandberg also stresses the importance of choosing the right person to set up house with and procreate, which goes both ways for both sexes. I love how Gloria Steinem remarked on Sandberg's advice: "She actually suggests that if men want children, they could also raise them!"

Sandberg struck a huge chord with her book's lofty agenda, but it also kept the conversation very one-sided. Kathleen Gerson, a sociologist at New York University and author of *The Unfinished Revolution*, asks a fundamental question: why do we continue to focus on the challenges of work-life balance as a women's issue, when the evidence clearly shows that it's shared by men? Gerson believes that we all harbor false ideas about the divide between men and women. As someone who has devoted her life to studying families, work, diversity, and how societies have behaved differently across various historical periods, she's come to the conclusion that the conversation shouldn't be about how women and men are "hard-wired differently." In fact she doesn't even believe in that idea. We can actually look back to moments in history when men—not women—were considered the most important parent, for they sustained the family financially. Whenever we mentally place women and men in separate categories, we put the word *all* in front of each group—as in "all women" and "all men." And in Gerson's perspective, this doesn't make sense.

"We know there's enormous variation among men and women," Gerson says, "but those are primarily probabilistic differences. I don't even believe women are better at some things than men. We're all individuals. The issue is what do we *value*, not how we are wired." She then goes on to assert that if we value a range of qualities, from being a well-rounded person to moving seamlessly between home and work commitments, then this will benefit men and women alike. It's not that there's an inherent asset or trait that women or, conversely, men lack. If you look throughout human history, every time doors have opened for women (usually by our own doing), we've walked through them with resolve and a sense of fulfillment. But stereotypes have followed us, too. And the same can be said for men as well. Gerson offers a good analogy: "Looking at gay parenting alone, we are forced to admit that the qualities we call human are not necessarily related to gender. There are qualities that each of us has the capacity to develop and use, and we have to decide how to use them."

I wholeheartedly agree: we should be focusing on values, not sexist stereotypes. It's imperative, in fact, as we watch an increasing number of couples negotiating their roles, such as whose career will take priority, under this new dynamic. While the share of married-couple families in which both parents worked was 59 percent in 2012, it's no longer a given that the man's job will take priority or that he'll sacrifice time with his family to pursue more money. In a poll taken in 2000 by the Radcliffe Public Policy Center asking men and women in their twenties whether they would accept a lower salary to spend more time with their families, 71 percent of the men answered yes, compared with 63 percent of the women. And since then, numerous other surveys, many of them conducted and published by Pew Research Center, have corroborated this trend. So men have been talking about wanting to be really involved fathers, expecting and assuming that their wives are going to be committed to their careers, for longer than we think. According to Michael Kimmel, a sociology professor at Stony Brook University who consults with companies around issues of gender equality, it's also true that the men who are in the workforce with these ambitions face the same challenges that women do.

Although we tend to think that the whole "work-life balance" conversation is primarily a women's issue, or that it's confined to working mothers in particular (cue the image of the slightly disheveled woman in a business suit juggling a babbling baby, laptop, laundry, and briefcase), interestingly enough there is some research that suggests men feel more conflict and have a greater desire for balance than women. A March 2013 Pew Research Center study about modern parenthood found that nearly equal proportions of parents were barely treading water trying to "do it all." Fifty percent of working fathers and 56 percent of working mothers found it "very" or "somewhat" difficult to balance work and family, while 48 percent of working fathers and 52 percent of working mothers responded that they'd prefer to be home with their children but needed to work for the income. Another study, done in 2008 by the Families and Work Institute, revealed even more dramatic numbers, finding that 60 percent of men in dual-income households admit to experiencing work-life conflict, versus 47 percent of women (reflecting a 35 percent increase from thirty years ago). In late 2013, a survey sponsored by LinkedIn and Citi that asked a little more than a thousand professionals about "having it all" revealed that 79 percent of men interpret that goal to include a "strong, loving marriage" while just 66 percent of women think the same. To my surprise, the small study found that men—much more so than women—include children in their definition of success (86 percent of men said that having kids is part of the "having it all" ideal versus just 73 percent of women). But for most women, the "having it all" picture still involves a thriving career, an enjoyable home life with children, and a fulfilling relationship or marriage. And not surprisingly, both sexes value work-life balance in fairly equal numbers, although a few more men (50 percent) than women (48 percent) call it a major concern.

It's not too far a stretch of the imagination to speculate why men seemingly feel more pressure today than ever before to balance work and family life. As women we've been adjusting our expectations and talking about work-life balance for a lot longer. We practically wrote the original "work-life balance" and "having it all" narrative that's now a constant topic for debate among both sexes, even though these phrases clearly mean different things to different people. The combination of changing roles for both men and women but a lack of support through workplace benefits and child care resources to keep up with these changes has forced the conversation among men who are now confronted with "either/ors" that women have been dealing with for a long time. They are now making the same kinds of sacrifices as women to live up to their ideal picture of "balance"—whatever that means.

I think it's fabulous that today men spend three times as much time with their children as their grandfathers did. But it's not so great that many employers and corporations haven't fully acknowledged this shift and made accommodations. In Gerson's words: "The gender revolution has really stalled when it comes to cultural views on men and options that men enjoy or don't. Men in general are caught between a rock and a hard place in which they're still expected to be the main earner, and if not, then they are seen as somehow not successful and possibly a failure. And this is a very tough road for men to go down. What it means is that in order to feel worthy of marriage and parenthood they feel the need to establish a solid base at work by devoting themselves to the office because our work institutions have become greedier than in the past. So, it's almost by default that they say 'If I'm going to live up to these standards, what choice do I have but to stress work over care taking and to leave the rest of the work, the less valued, less rewarded work, to my partner?' It isn't that men prefer this or want this. It's that the cultural standards, the pressures, the institutional pressures on them make it very difficult to see a way toward a more egalitarian partnership."

According to Gerson's research, the vast majority of young people in the United States—about 80 percent of women and 70 percent of men between the ages of eighteen and thirty-two across all races, classes, and family backgrounds—want an egalitarian marriage. By "egalitarian," we're talking about a relationship in which both partners share pretty much everything equally, from the income generating to the housekeeping and child rearing. In practice, however, such relationships are difficult to establish. Both work and family are, in Gerson's summation, "greedy institutions." They take up lots of time and energy. And many couples find that, once children arrive, it's impossible for each individual to do both with equal gusto. One person usually has to take a step back professionally to focus more on the child care, which in the past has been the woman. So today's world of breadwinning wives and moms creates an added challenge, as the fallback strategy (Dad works, Mom cares) is no longer viable. Those who do achieve an equal balance in their relationship (and commitments to work and family) aren't necessarily enjoying it or "thriving." They often feel like salmon swimming upstream. They're doing it, but without much help and support from social and corporate structures. And that needs to change in this new fairy tale.

I appreciate how the author of another *Atlantic* article, this one penned by a man, Stephen Marche, married to a breadwinning woman, stated it when he said work-life balance will only improve once we involve men and realize they don't get to "have it all," either. They should speak up and ask for paternity leave, especially since employers are more likely to listen to them than to women, sadly. In his words: "As long as family issues are miscast as women's issues, they will be dismissed as the pleadings of one interest group among many." He then illustrated his point by bringing up a valid comparison: when gay rights activists went from focusing on their rights as an oppressed minority to simply addressing their struggle to create and support families, their movement finally had a chance to succeed and win politically. Marche is right: "It is easy to have a career as an anti-feminist. Force the opponents of day-care support and family leave to come out instead against working families. Let them try to sell that."

"Lean In" to Your Relationships

Whether or not you side with Gerson's call to action from a broader, societal perspective or Sandberg's dictum for individual women, and whether or not you strive to "have it all," the good news is that as women making more, we have an opportunity to author our own script and fairy tale. We can change our personal and social standards plus the collective narrative for good. As we toss gender roles in the air and see how they fall, the conversation begs to be put on the table. I think we all can agree that we need to redefine marital and familial contribution, as well as rethink what it means to be a "provider" and what it means to be "feminine" or "masculine" in relationships. And we must turn all these conversations about "women and money" into ones about "families and money."

And this, my friends, is what rewriting the fairy tale is all about. We need to rewrite the rules.

So forget about what our moms told us would happen or what society says we should do. That bill of goods has expired. And let's ditch the idea that women have to be the ladies of the house, that we should feel badly about making more money than our men, or that our roles are dictated in stone. The reality is that we're holding the wallet, and that's quite a powerful and status-changing place to be. We can still experience the fairy tale, but it'll be a new one as written and told by us, with new rules about not only money but relationships.

In your quest to rewrite your own fairy tale, one thing to keep in mind is that as individual women, we each look for different things in our relationships. Some of us want to be swept off our feet the old-fashioned way. Some want to be taken care of. Some want to retain traditional, housewifery roles despite our moneymaking prowess. Some of us don't mind having a messy house and have husbands who get a free pass on cleaning, while others believe that the way you maintain your home is important and, to quote a friend of mine, that "a man who manages twelve people at work, meets deadlines, and has a college degree can pick up his socks and place clothes in the washer." And some of us do strive for an equal partnership, even if that means making more of the money while your man does his fair share in another area of your life together. Very few women will say they are looking for a husband to keep as a kind of pet. But if he is not pulling his weight—and there are many ways not to pull your weight—what kind of dynamic do you have? It's not an impossible situation, but you really have to pay attention and not dust it off as the new way of the world.

If you're ambitious enough to "lean in" all the way toward your career and income potential, how much are you willing to "lean in" to your relationship and make it work? If you're among the women who are in a relationship with a man whose self-esteem is lower when he sees you succeed than when he sees you fail, how can your relationship survive? (No less of an authority than the American Psychological Association found this to be true among many men when it reported on a new study, from researchers at the University of Florida and the University of Virginia, that men not only experience a blow to their self-esteem when their female partners experience success—even when they aren't in direct competition—but that women's success also negatively affects how men view the future of the relationship!) As we saw with Michelle and Carmen, as well as in the cautionary statistics for breadwinning women in affair-prone relationships, these new dynamics always come with their own sets of complications.

Unfortunately, the idea of "leaning in" to one's relationship seems to be a low priority for young women today. In 2013, the *New York Times* reported on the modern "hookup culture" led by "hard-charging and ambitious young women" at elite universities. For those of you who need clarification: hooking up generally refers to casual sex without emotional obligations to commence a relationship (it can also just refer to making out or engaging in sexual acts with the exception of intercourse). Frankly, it's sad to think that young women (myself once included) are abandoning the art of relationship building in exchange for hooking up. A strong, happy relationship rarely happens serendipitously, and if young women delay dating to the point that they refuse to enter a serious relationship for fear it can muck up their career ambitions, then they'll be lucky to find a suitable match by the time they're forty and their biological clock's alarm is ringing. And when they don't find a suitable partner, they may well regret having used their youthful years just pushing relentlessly to get their degrees and superdegrees.

I dare say there is some truth to the letter Susan Patton, a

Princeton alumna and mother, wrote to the *Daily Princetonian* about the importance of investing time and energy in meeting Mr. Right in college. In her letter, she stated her perspective in a no-holds-barred tone: "For most of you, the cornerstone of your future and happiness will be inextricably linked to the man you marry, and you will never again have this concentration of men who are worthy of you." While her recommendation may have come across as insulting and obsolete—a return to a bygone era when many women went to college for their "M.R.S." degree, I nonetheless find some value in her appeal. Someone like Hanna Rosin, the author of *The End of Men*, would say that this modern lifestyle among young women is simply a "functional strategy," a way for them to enjoy their sex lives without wasting precious energy on building and maintaining real relationships with their sex partners. But in my view, this can have long-term consequences that can lead to deep, irrepressible regrets later in life.

In my family, dating was taboo. I almost wasn't even allowed to go to the prom because my parents considered it a trashy American ritual where teen girls got knocked up. I suppose my parents assumed that I would randomly meet my handsome Prince Charming while buying coffee or shopping at the grocery store one day. When Mom called me in college to catch up, I never spoke of the boys I was dating. My fear of ever having to tell my parents that I had a boyfriend made me feel a little bit of shame, as if I would be letting some silly romance distract me from the *real* reason I went to college: to get an education. It feels like a miracle that I found love and got married to such an amazing man.

Maybe you'll think this is crazy, but I remember turning twenty-six and sitting on a park bench in New York. My mom had called me earlier that day to wish me a happy birthday and tell me it was a "spiritual day" and that I should make a wish because it would come true. So I did just that as I sat there. After a string of failed mini relationships over the previous few years, and being reluctant to date online, I resorted to the irrational: "making a wish." And so it was on this park bench on the Upper West Side that I wished and prayed and begged to find a nice guy who would appreciate and love me. A few months later I reconnected with Tim after several years apart. Coincidence? I guess there was some serendipity in that, but, of course, not every girl can depend on luck to meet Mr. Right. Just as you need to put time and effort into building and maintaining a thriving career, you need to do the same in your romantic life. The only exception to this rule is if you truly never plan to be in a serious relationship, let alone get married and have kids.

Money and Marriage Aren't Everything

Although marriage isn't everything, most can agree that having satisfying, healthy relationships that add to our sense of self and ability to be successful in whatever we choose to do factors mightily into our quality of life. Family therapist and social philosopher Michael Gurian reminds us that regardless of money issues, one of the most important reasons for engaging in relationships at all is to help one another fulfill our life's purpose. A lot of couples spend far too much time trying to change each other's personality, only to end up denigrating each other (and having extramarital affairs). While we tend to think of marriage in romantic terms, that's not what it was originally intended for. For centuries it's been an institution that merely facilitated survival, and in today's world we can translate that to mean helping one another figure out reasons for living. In the new fairy tale we write, we female breadwinners must approach our relationships with this in mind. It behooves us to look at our mates as partners in our success—regardless of their own income.

Gurian also encourages us to think of our lives in terms of stages, which can be enormously helpful in weathering the inevitable storms that come in different decades or stages in life. As I've already mentioned, how a twenty-something thinks and behaves will naturally be different from the way someone in the latter half of life does. This reality has also inspired Emma Johnson, a divorcée back in the dating world and a blogger at WealthySingle Mommy.com, to propose an innovative idea: a "10-year marriage contract" that lays out the goals and spells out the expectations of the relationship and can be renewed (and changed) every decade. She cites a good reason: study after study finds that a lack of communication is the number one reason people divorce (also true of relationships in which the woman makes more). "A forced conversation about the future of a marriage can only be good for any relationship," Johnson says. "Gone will be the days of the couch potato marriage, where everyone simply waits out the clock without actually working on the relationship."

Similarly, Adam Gilad, former Stanford University Graduate Research Fellow and a top relationship expert, advocates the need for a "relationship constitution." In drafting it, start with the "why" of the relationship. He instructs: "Discuss why you're in an intimate relationship. People don't do this. They lurch into it and hope for the best." Next, Gilad says to commit to behaviors, not feelings. "One of the most idiotic things we do [when we get married] is to say, 'I promise on this day to feel a certain way for the rest of my life.' That's absurd. Instead, be committed to building and serving the love between you and your mate. Commit to actions and roles that serve the health and happiness of your life together." Also key in Gilad's teachings: be open to making amendments to the constitution much more frequently, in fact, than Johnson's marriage contract. According to Gilad, "It's very important . . . that you change the plan. Look at it every six months. Is it serving the love between us? [If not,] how can we amend it? Don't get caught up on 'Well, you said three years ago . . . !' You have to flow."

When Michael Gurian counsels couples in crisis, one of the first exercises he has them do is write out their individual anxieties. He also has them each make two lists, one that itemizes what he or she is doing that's *essential to the partnership* and another that lists what he or she is doing that's *essential to his or her individual self*. And then Gurian shows them where they are lopsided. This could be a useful exercise to do for anyone hoping to take her relationship to the next level. Later on, we'll see how Gurian explains why men have more to bring to the table than they realize, and it has nothing to do with housework. "The pivot for equality is not about power," he asserts.

Communication has always been key to any relationship, but it's even more important in those where she makes more. I can't reiterate this enough, for when I drill down all the data and anecdotal evidence, the message is clear: if you can keep the lines of communication open in your relationship, you stand a much greater chance of making it work and avoiding what's arguably the most dangerous home wrecker of all—resentment.

Calling All Single Girls: Live by the Rules on the First Date

For all you single women out there looking for love (possibly in all the wrong places) listen up. I know how hard it can be to find the right guy when you're financially independent. Many men can easily be intimidated by a woman's success, especially when her success means she doesn't need a man's money. Fiercely independent Chelsea is the perfect example of someone whose income negatively affects her dating life. Forty-five years old, she paid for her master's degree herself and works as a television producer and writer in Toronto, where she makes six figures and owns a condo that will be paid off in five years. A recent date boldly told her that it bothered him that she didn't need him to be the provider. I think any man who thinks like that probably wouldn't be good for her in the long run anyhow. But his admission highlights the gender-based roles that some men still abide by. And it's something that any financially independent woman needs to be on the lookout for. Chelsea adds: "It's funny because it always starts out great. Guys love the fact that you're independent, busy with your career and your friends, and that you have a lot going on. At the beginning of the relationship it's appealing because you're not clingy. But then they get more serious and want more of your time and what was attractive initially becomes a liability—a fault. You're not needy enough, and that becomes a problem."

Melanie Notkin, forty-three, shares a lament similar to Chelsea's, albeit from another angle that concerns many forty-something women. Single and successful as the founder of the international brand SavvyAuntie.com, an online destination for childless women who love kids and their role playing auntie or godmother, Melanie is also the author of *Otherhood*, which looks at "the unrequited love of [her] generation." In it she features interviews with dozens of men and women who have been searching for love to no avail. For the single women, in particular, who are approaching forty, they're concerned about not only finding love, but finding motherhood, as well. The Centers for Disease Control and Prevention reports that of the nearly 20 percent of women who remain childless between the ages of forty and forty-four, half are childfree by choice. And while there are many reasons for making that choice, I can't help but wonder how much of the remaining 10 percent is composed of high-earning women who didn't find the right guy and whose dating life was negatively affected by her success. Although more and more women today are choosing to have kids on their own if they don't meet Mr. Right by forty years old, there are still a good number of financially independent women who let time (and opportunities) go by and who find themselves childless at fifty. I whisked Melanie away one Sunday afternoon for a cocktail so she could share with me her insights into dating, men, and why some single women need to be much more "generous" in how they size up their potential mates.

Melanie has built a large, diverse community serving an "Auntourage" of childless women as a result of choosing to look at her life differently. (There are about twenty-three million women in the United States who are potentially in this category and they are, on average, thirty-six years old. More than half of them have never been married and 34 percent have an annual household income of $50,000 or more.) It wasn't an easy journey for her to reach the realization that being a single, childless woman was actually the right path for her. As she describes in her book and in an essay posted on the *Huffington Post*, she started to "suffer the prejudice of being an 'older' woman" without a husband or kids while in her midthirties. From various men and potential suitors she's been told that she's past her prime for the dating world and that she should consider freezing her eggs.

These experiences deeply affected Melanie. We talked about how our generation of thirty- and forty-something women is the first to have more choices in life that facilitate waiting for love rather than having to settle for financial reasons. We can take care of ourselves, but sometimes that choice can affect whether or not we have children. Now forty-two, Melanie has accepted the fact she probably won't have biological children of her own. And she has no regrets.

When I asked Melanie what a single successful girl is supposed
to do, she said that even when financially independent women target men they *think* will be more accepting of a woman's success,
ambition, and drive, that's hardly the case. There's a tendency, according to her, for breadwinning women to think an older man
will do. But older men can in fact be more traditional. In her view,
a lot of men—especially the older ones—want to feel looked up to.
We have to be much more generous with how we help men feel
good about themselves, despite their income. Melanie also believes
that, age aside, men in general have an inherent need to quantify
their work, but this is hard to appreciate if they're making the same
or less than their partner. Which is why women dating or partner-
ing with men at any age who make less need to look beyond income as a source of attraction. Melanie gravitates toward male
entrepreneurs old and young. "When a man decides to take a risk
and do something on his own, even if he isn't making any money,
that's more attractive than a man who has a steady job but is unhappy."

For those who are contemplating children, either biologically
or through adoption, you need to discuss this openly with the person you're choosing to be a life partner—no matter his age. Don't
be shy about it. And don't think that you have to compromise. It's
not enough to just find Mr. Right. You need to find the kind of Mr.
Right who will want to be a parent with you (if that's important to
you). I think sometimes, as women, we're willing to make serious
trade-offs just to win the love of a man. It's like work. We're so
happy to have the job that we fail to ask for a raise, better benefits,
or the corner office. Take my friend Lauren, whose boyfriend of
nearly seven years has convinced her that they don't need to get
married. He doesn't believe in the concept and actually refuses to
attend her friends' marriage ceremonies. He also has convinced
her that they don't "need to exchange gifts." Why? He doesn't be-

lieve in giving presents as a show of affection. "But he would die for me!" Lauren gushes. But love, I reckon, doesn't conquer all. I can tell she's clearly bothered by his stubbornness and feels neglected in big ways, though she seems to be settling because, well, he "loves" her.

Don't Settle

One lesson that Melanie has learned through her work with high-earning women is never to settle or, God forbid, take a step back to lure men. She's met many women who regret leaving high-powered careers years ago in the hopes they could attract men who wouldn't be intimidated by their success or who wouldn't find their profession competitive with theirs. But sadly, many of these women never found the love they were seeking, and now they are far behind where they would have been professionally (and financially) if they had stayed on track with their career ambitions.

But Melanie isn't a fan of the whole "leaning in" mantra. She thinks it sends women the wrong signal that they need to be manly in the way they approach work. She tells me, "This whole idea of leaning in is very masculine. . . . Leaning out is feminine." And she gestures "leaning out" by sitting calmly back in her seat and staring me in the eyes, as if to say, "I'm relaxed; I'm confident; and I'm listening." From her perspective, as women we're given contradictory messages. On the one hand we're told to work hard, make good money, and be our own caregiver. But on the other hand society still expects us to get married, have children, and be nurturing. So there's a lot of pressure on us. Some of this pressure, however, can deflate when we realize that there's an enormous community of women who are defying expectations and finding happiness in other ways—through friendships, nieces, nephews, and careers.

So I say, if you're choosing not to be on the path that includes marriage and children, then lock into that childless community and live freely. That said, I should add that "waiting for your equal" (something I hear a lot from my single girlfriends) can too often mean waiting for someone who's proven to be as ambitious and successful as you, which is just setting yourself up for perpetual singlehood. You might be better off changing your definition of "equal." According to relationship coach and founder of Dating withDignity.com Marni Battista, "A guy who doesn't make as much, maybe he's less competitive but just passionate about what he does. He's going to more easily jump into her life. He's going to make her more happy. He's going to be more agreeable."

Melanie Notkin isn't the only woman I interviewed who is put off by the concept of leaning in, but I think that we can argue for or against it depending on how one defines the term. I'm not entirely sure Sandberg herself would say that she wants women to act more like men. But semantics aside, one truth about our lives today is that we can be "naïve and idealistic" amid all the recent turns of events. And this is where Sandberg gets it right when discussing how her generation was raised in an era of increasing equality: "Integrating professional and personal aspirations proved far more challenging than we had imagined. During the same years that our career demanded maximum time investment, our biology demanded that we have children. Our partners did not share the housework and child rearing, so we found ourselves with two full-time jobs. The workplace did not evolve to give us the flexibility we needed to fulfill our responsibilities at home. We anticipated none of this. We were caught by surprise."

Caught by surprise is putting it mildly. The fact that a breadwinning woman in particular creates a powerful, undeniable dynamic that unexpectedly affects the daily life of both sexes—regardless of marriage, age, culture, progeny, ambitions, and social status—brings us to the obvious question: what guidelines should we follow in re-writing this fairy tale for the sake of our own survival and happi-ness? How are we going to remove the barriers that prevent women like us from enjoying success in our relationships as much as we thrive in our work? How can we avoid any more surprises if we're going to continue this trend? And how can those of us who are al-ready knee-deep in a serious relationship, and perhaps already have kids, do some backpedaling to fix problems that have been brewing, maybe for a long time?

Answer: start to rewrite the fairy tale as soon as possible and incorporate the remaining eight rules into your life right away as you see fit. Once you've embraced the first two orders of business—facing the facts and accepting a new story line—it's time to execute. And engage.

Initiate and Go Full Monty

If you're already in the thick of a committed relationship, then you and your man are already well aware of any existing income dis-parities. But I do have to start somewhere and briefly address those who are not yet playing house and who don't know how to broach the subject of finances in the dating world. So for all you gals start-ing relationships, listen up. This section is for you.

You're more likely to get yourself into trouble if you keep infor-mation (secrets) from your potential suitor on the very first date. Imagine a couple who begin dating and she doesn't allude to what she does, consistently devalues herself, and insists she earns a modest salary (which, incidentally, is what a male coworker of mine more or less suggested I do in my early twenties after a num-ber of dates with alpha men that led to nowhere). After a month or two, they start getting serious, and she finds herself unable to divulge her net worth because she's already lied about her assets. Eventually the truth comes out but it's now much more painful for him. He wonders what else she has been lying about, and the relationship is founded on shaky ground. Not only does he experience an immense loss of trust, but he may also lose confidence in himself and feel ashamed. Why? Two possible reasons: he thought he made more or he believes that she didn't have enough confidence in him to share what she really earned. Obviously this can create a complex web of hurt feelings, jealousy, distrust, guilt, and lack of communication.

So leave nothing to the imagination about your financial standing. Never downplay your earnings, which is a mistake made by far too many women. When high-profile real estate broker and contributor for NBC's *Today* show Barbara Corcoran netted more money than her husband one year, she pretended it was an accounting error. "By the time the third year hit, I was earning five times more than he was and it was obvious we had to adjust to the reality," she said for a feature article in *New York* magazine.

When Tim and I swapped the state of our financial affairs over margaritas that summer afternoon when we first started dating, I acted coy about my gross income for the year. In addition to my salary, I had a sizable book advance that I had initially left out of the conversation. It was Tim who asked, "Does this income include your book advance and year-end bonus?"

Good thing he didn't see me blush. "Oh, yeah . . . heh, heh," I said. It was stupid to beat around the bush because it had pushed Tim to probe further. He sensed a little dishonesty, which could have made him question my overall integrity and fortitude. But I didn't want to come across as miles apart financially from him. This kind of chicanery or "untruthfulness" can backfire.

According to psychologist Brad Klontz, "Women may self-sabotage . . . because they feel being totally honest might threaten their relationship . . . the truth may chase their man away." My thinking at the time, however, was that if I admitted to making so much more, I'd hurt his feelings. I thought I'd come across as someone who was winning more than him in life (hence the higher income), which is not a healthy perspective to have in any relationship. It's not about scorekeeping based on income. Yes, I am (and maybe you are, too) competitive by nature, but I never want to be or feel competitive with my husband. And we can't ignore the fact that money is money. What you earn is sometimes just a factor of what your industry or company is willing to pay you. It doesn't mean you work harder or have a more meaningful job. It doesn't imply you're smarter or better at negotiating a salary. It doesn't convey that you went to a better school or are more "ambitious" or have stronger skills. It is what it is. A neurosurgeon will always make more than a kindergarten teacher, but both bear equal weight in so many more important categories than money. Be bold and up-front about your income in the very beginning and use his response to test how comfortable he is with the situation.

And be prepared: your guy may not be okay when he hears about the financial disparity. Wouldn't you like to know now before you get fully entangled? A gorgeous, successful TV anchor friend of mine recalled dating a mechanic back when she was a local news reporter. She made more than he did and had no debt. A total catch, right? Wrong. "It was a definite issue for him because he was always talking about how he had a mortgage and I had no such assets." He was trying to make a big deal out of the fact that he owned a house, just to serve his ego. Despite his undermining ways, she stayed with him for two years before realizing she was in a relationship that made her feel like total crap. "I allowed myself to stay with someone who constantly demeaned my profession and my accomplishments," she confessed. "Now I'm constantly trying to remind myself to really own my success. I worked hard to get where I am."

Bottom line: no one needs to brag about what they do and regale someone with all of their accomplishments on the first date. Talking all about work, work, work and how you just got promoted and blah, blah, blah, blah on the first date is not smart (same goes for men!). Don't lie or hide information but don't make that all you talk about, either. After all, you're a woman with a lot more to offer than ambition. Talk about family, travel, and your hobbies and passions. Sometimes men need to be eased into your financially independent world. Pace yourselves!

But when the topic comes up, couples benefit more from total transparency and respect than from the alternative. It's best to work out any resentments and difficulties related to the female earning more in the relationship sooner rather than later. The more you conceal your spending power early on, the harder it will be to come clean. And here's some icing for your cake: if you're a single mom banking beaucoup bucks and trying to date online, consider posting your income. Obviously, proceed with caution here, as this won't be for everyone. But it might work in your favor, so long as letting the world know your general income level won't come back to haunt you later in your industry or among colleagues. You might not have anything to lose but a hot date.

Emma Johnson, the woman who came up with the idea of a ten-year marriage contract, did just that after not finding guys she was interested in to date. As soon as she disclosed her six-figure income, quality men started to contact her. "I'm a single mom and freelance writer," she told me. "If that doesn't scream poverty, I don't know what does. The divorced guys I date love the fact that I'm financially independent because they're so pissed their ex-wives stayed at home, so pissed they're paying child support. And in their opinion they think, 'She was lazy. I wanted her to get a job. I didn't want her to stay at home.'"

THREE TELLTALE SIGNS YOU'RE WITH MR. WRONG

- *Sarcasm*: According to my interview with Eileen Gallo, a psychotherapist in Los Angeles who runs a family clinic with her husband, Jon Gallo, women must watch out for sarcastic comments early on in the relationship about her lifestyle, her income, or her interests. "If you're wearing a new dress and he can only talk about how much money it cost, that's an Aha! warning," she says. When relationship coach Marni Battista was single, she used to invite first dates to her big, beautiful home in Los Angeles to pick her up. Based on some reactions or remarks, she was able to identify the men who were likely insecure with her financial independence. "I remember a guy picked me up and walked in . . . and he said, 'Wow, nice house! Hope you don't ever expect me to pay the mortgage on this thing!' If a guy is going to say that, he's not confident. He's not secure," she says.
- *Undermining*: Ever get the feeling that your guy doesn't think your job's that important? Carmen recalls how David would react to her ambitions to become an actress when they first met. "When he first met me I was an actress and he thought, 'Oh, how cute! Isn't that more like a hobby?' I said, 'No, it's what I do for a living.'"
- *Pointing out your nonexistent financial "flaws"*: If you make more money but don't drive a fancy car or own a home, and your man (who earns less) constantly points out the fact that he has a lot of "assets" (car, home, big-screen TV, etc.), then that's a red flag. Your income, after all, is an asset—much more so than his toys and bank loans.

Be Clear About What It Means
to Be "Ambitious"

Any woman in a committed relationship reading this today is likely asking, *Did I choose wisely?* Here's the gist of what one hardworking woman said when she sounded off online upon asking herself this very question: "I've been trying to get my man to get a second job, and instead he likes to stay out late and sleep in before his shift. I make significantly more than he does, but that's not what's bothering me. It's the fact I usually work sixty hours a week, and I'm freaking tired of being the only person (seemingly) making an effort! This, after a year-plus of him cycling between being unemployed, having a crap job for a few months, and then getting fired for something really stupid. I'm starting to feel like it's just not worth it. I put myself in crazy debt this past year paying for him to move in with me (from another state) and he can't even get out of bed to get a second job? I LOVE him, but I feel taken advantage of and my little angry-Annie-on-the-inside is stomping her feet with steam coming out of her ears."

This brings up a good question every breadwinning woman needs to ask herself in rewriting her script: what does ambition mean to you? Maybe you're fine with a husband who covers more of the child care and works part-time. And maybe you're not. At the end of the day, we all know that it's not always about the money. It's about values and our definition of things like integrity, ambition, motivation, and purpose. A man who is not making the same amount as you is immediately stripped of traditional masculinity, and for many women that void begs to be filled in some significant way. Otherwise, it's easy for a man to come off as lazy if he's not bringing home the bigger paycheck.

In addition to encouraging couples in crisis to write out their anxieties about the relationship and share them, Michael Gurian also advises that they focus on what he calls "criticality," a concept I think is exceptionally useful for breadwinning women already in a committed partnership who feel like they've made mistakes (and/or their partner has) and they want to remedy problems in lieu of divorce. What tends to happen, according to Gurian, is that one person in the relationship is anxious but may not realize it, and that anxiety can lead to being very critical of the other person. If you can identify and acknowledge each other's anxieties that stimulate the verbal aggressions ("criticalities"), then you have a doorway through which you can work on the relationship and rewrite that script.

Another doorway Gurian likes to use is the concept of purpose, as I described earlier. In many relationships in which she makes more, the guy doesn't feel needed. He's also often unable to express what's going on in his head. In Gurian's words: "She has the expectation that he should be able to express what's going on, and she not only has that expectation but begins to shame him or be hypercritical. And that could be a killer. That's death for anyone." Gurian adds that if a man doesn't feel needed *and* he's getting shamed and criticized . . . this is a core problem to work on. So you have to start with this question: who feels needed and who doesn't? That can be a starter mental exercise for rewriting your fairy tale. Then take the exercise further in a more practical manner, by doing what Gurian has his clients do: make a list of those individual anxieties alongside what each person finds essential to the partnership and to the self and begin to create solutions based on where there are obvious discrepancies or gaps. These solutions can be any number of things, from outsourcing more housework to having him take care of the annual taxes (logistically speaking) while you cover the general bill paying. This in turn should help reorient how you speak to one another, as well as how you continue to rewrite your fairy tale.

Fair warning: this isn't something that gets done in a day or even a month. Gurian cautions that such work is ongoing; it takes about a year before you can really get to the root of all the issues hidden in the human psyche and be equipped to address deep-seated fears, anxieties, and criticalities.

Not all fairy tales have to read the same. My narrative will be different from yours. The key is to make sure that whatever fairy tale you write today, given your unique circumstances, you stay honest and truthful to yourself. This, in turn, will send a powerful message to your partner and encourage him to participate in the relationship according to your expectations, needs, and desires. Of course, his fairy tale will change, too, from traditional norms. Remember, fairy tales are, by definition, fictional and fantastical, which is why our rewrite has to essentially create a whole new genre for us; it has to be a story that reflects our innate cravings for our men to be men while honoring this new reality in our financial lives. And it's all possible if you commit to abandoning some traditions as you establish new ones.

Finally, ask yourself: is it his lack of money—or his lack of effort? Again, it helps to be honest with yourself about how you define ambition and how it plays into your relationship's dynamics.

RULE #2 RECAP

+ Under this new dynamic, each one of us female bread-winners has to rewrite our fairy tale—the story of our lives and how we choose to live it in terms of expectations, goals, and the things that make us happy and fulfilled in our relationships.
+ Men are not immune to the challenges; they, too, strive to "have it all" in egalitarian relationships and achieve "work-life balance" but face the same lack of support in

corporate and social settings. Their fairy tale is changing, too.

- The "lean in" mantra of today isn't just about work and career ambitions. In our new fairy tale, to get the happy ending we all want, we need to lean in to all that we do—at work, at home, and especially in our romantic relationships. Although some like to think the lean-in movement is masculine, it doesn't have to be. We can leverage the concept to mean that we fully engage actively in all facets of our lives.

- Take ownership of your income from day one in the dating world. Don't hide the facts. Be honest and transparent even if you fear intimidating a man on the first date. Otherwise, you won't find Mr. Right and might end up with Mr. Wrong.

- You get to define what it means to be ambitious and how that plays into what kind of partner you want and need. Can you be with someone who dials back his career ambitions to support your career and perhaps be the primary parent at home? Or do you prefer someone who has clear professional goals and strives to achieve them no matter what?

- For those already in a committed relationship who need to rewrite their fairy tale, start with questions about your and your partner's anxieties and criticalities. What makes you anxious in the relationship? When and why are you critical of your partner? Who feels needed and who doesn't? How can you remedy all this through practical solutions? The answers to these important questions will give you the tools you need to rewrite your personal narrative. But be realistic: these rewrites take time and patience. Give yourself at least a year.

CHAPTER 3

Rule #3: Level the Financial Playing Field

Part of the allure to the hit show *Mad Men* is watching a bygone era—the time when men made all the money and worked all the hours. Women did their part for the household by making sure the children were cared for, the kitchen was stocked, meals were prepared, the laundry was done, the checkbook was balanced, and all the metaphorical family-related trains ran on time all year long. The few women who took on jobs as secretaries and office managers still wore the housewife hat at home. In general, he made, she spent, and successful couples ran the household like a partnership.

Today, not only has this dynamic been shaken up by women taking on leadership roles in the workforce, but it's made for an interesting turn of events with regard to which person is likely to make financial decisions. Studies show that in most households where the husband earns more money, both spouses share in the financial decision making. But in marriages where the wife brings home a bigger paycheck, the woman is *twice* as likely as her husband to make all the financial decisions. The survey I conducted with Brad Klontz confirmed this trend. We asked our participants—more than one thousand heterosexual women in committed relationships, a little more than half of whom make more than their mate—who was responsible for managing various financial matters. Here's what we found (note that the numbers reflect the percentage of women we surveyed from each camp—one in which she makes less and the other in which she makes more—who take control of these various responsibilities in their relationship; so, for instance, 62 percent of the women who make more take responsibility for paying bills whereas only 43 percent of the women who earn less take charge of that financial chore):

	WHEN SHE MAKES LESS	WHEN SHE MAKES MORE
PAYING BILLS	43%	62%
MONITORING SPENDING	45%	56%
DECIDING ON PURCHASES	19%	26%
BUDGETING	42%	59%
SAVING	39%	59%
INVESTMENT DECISIONS	27%	44%
BRINGING UP CONVERSATIONS ABOUT MONEY	43%	56%
PLANNING FOR RETIREMENT	31%	54%

Evidently, if you make more than your man, you're more likely to be the primary decision maker on money matters and take charge of things like paying bills, budgeting, saving, and planning for retirement. But such an arrangement could be asking for trouble—it calls for a new rule.

A sense of equity between two committed people is important, even if there's an income disparity. But for a man to keep his dignity and sense of engagement, he needs to feel that he plays an important role in the relationship and that he's not completely isolated from the financial decisions. And for a woman to keep her sanity and sex drive alive, she shouldn't have to do the equivalent of a CFO's job (for free!) after she's gotten home from the nine to five (or seven to eleven).

Consider this scenario: When Kyle lost his job in IT in 2011, his social worker wife Lily suddenly became the breadwinner for their family of six. The Houston couple's income shrank by 50 percent, but their bills continued to pour in. The stress was mounting, so Lily took it upon herself to manage all of the family's finances (i.e., paying bills, balancing the checkbook, managing the savings account) while Kyle buried himself in his job search. It felt like she was helping out—why saddle Kyle with more work when he could be polishing his resume and practicing his interview skills? But in taking over the finances, Lily cut Kyle out of the decision-making process. Yes, she took care of the bills and bought the groceries, but she also did not appreciate when her husband used their discretionary money to buy, say, a new pair of golf shoes. And thus a vicious cycle was born: Kyle, grasping for some sense of autonomy and dignity, started making (and hiding) personal purchases outside of the budget. Lily then clamped down tighter. Each started to lose respect for the other.

The challenge: How can men and women help each other not just *feel* accountable but *be* accountable for their finances when she makes more? From a practical standpoint, who pays for the mortgage, vacations, and everyday living expenses? From an emotional standpoint, how do you make him feel like a player and that his contributions—financial or otherwise—matter? What steps can a couple take to reach financial fairness? Although he may not make as much, how can he feel as involved with and connected to their shared financial life as she is? The answer lies in following Rule #3: level the financial playing field. In every relationship the solutions are different and no one way is necessarily right or wrong, as long as both of you are on the same page and agree to the protocols.

Running a household is akin to running a business, and you have to know what your priorities, expectations, and responsibilities are. This helps build the trust that's key to a healthy relationship. If you're not straightforward and outspoken about how you and your partner are going to share the bill paying and make financial decisions, then that personal enterprise can turn sour and incite many negative emotions in both of you very quickly. Which is why Rule #3 involves not only figuring out which payment strategy works best for you and your partner, depending on your comfort levels, but, more than anything, figuring out how to communicate effectively, manage inevitable imbalances, and address the war-prone areas crouching deep in your heart that have everything to do with the most fractious of feelings—pride, respect, self-confidence and self-perceived adequacy, autonomy and sense of independence, and even shame and envy. All of these emotions vigorously compete against one another to some extent when it comes to money, and any one of them can spell trouble or even become the death knell to a relationship if it drives insurmountable negativity.

This chapter outlines my essential tips to navigating this tough terrain when you make more. And we'll start with the functional— how to pick a payment strategy—and then we'll move to the grittier details of negotiating all the emotional baggage wrapped up in each of your roles on a daily basis.

Get on Top (of Your Emotions)

I'm assuming that by the time you're having a heart-to-heart conversation about covering bills, you and your partner have a clear picture of who makes what. After all, when the relationship becomes serious (i.e., you move in together, get married, or otherwise become life partners) and you begin to share expenses and goals, naturally you'll need to figure out how to structure your finances. Contrary to what's implied by "pick a payment strategy," this isn't about choosing Visa, MasterCard, check, or cash. Nor is this decision as easy. Begin the process by doing a financial audit as well as an *emotional* audit. The financial inventory calculates how much each of you earns, what expenses you share, your respective debt levels, and so on. The emotional side of the equation helps you figure out who is best capable of taking the reins and managing the bills, as well as what kind of payment arrangement suits your needs and, let's be honest, your egos. If you need an opening line to use, try this one: "So tell me about your mother."

Talk About Your Mothers

There's a reason why a psychotherapist will often start by asking about a person's mother, as it often leads to a ton of useful information. One way of getting to know what you're emotionally okay with, in terms of who pays what and how, is by having several candid conversations about the role money played in your childhood. This goes for both you and your partner. What images remain stuck in your head from watching your parents handle money and bills as you grew up? For me, I had my fill of witnessing multiple men at various times fighting over the bill at a restaurant. For you, perhaps it was watching your mom work overtime to afford your school field trip. All of us have established a frame of reference from our upbringing, and this is especially true in matters of money; how your own mother made money (or didn't) has had an indelible impact on you whether you like it or not.

Come to grips with how that history has shaped your mind-set as an adult. Accept that your beliefs, impressions, and judgments about money have molded your current perception of reality and that they will evolve with new experiences. And be open to adopting other ideas in the future. For this reason, it's important to have *several* conversations because it's not practical or realistic to have just one and expect to resolve all the issues. Life tends to jog your memory and you will discover different understandings along the way. When you have these recalls, share them with each other. That's how Tim and I learned (and continue to learn) about each other's perspectives.

We travel down memory lane a lot trading stories. And we don't shy away from telling each other about, say, the time when I came home from college and my mom was in tears, lamenting that she was terrified because she didn't know how the money was getting managed. Back then my dad didn't involve my mom with the big-picture financials of the household. She didn't know how the mortgage got paid. She didn't know how much was parked in savings. It dawned on her one day (which coincided with me visiting during school break) that if something happened to my dad, she'd be utterly lost. I suppose that's part of my context for why I work as hard as I do to protect my finances and maximize my earnings. History matters. If you (or your partner) have only been exposed to a life where the man supports the family and the woman tends to domestic responsibilities, take note: it's a part of you (or your partner). You may respect some of it while having issues with other aspects of traditional arrangements, but don't ignore those rooted feelings. Make your own set of rules by factoring in features of your history that you and your partner are comfortable upholding. My Persian brain, for instance, is used to seeing the man take charge of the bill, so when we're at a restaurant, Tim uses the joint credit card that I pay in full every month. It may sound utterly ridiculous to some, but for me, it's like a public display of affection. And when we are with my family, it's comforting for my parents to see Tim settle a bill, too. I guess this is, in some weird way, our performance. Tim and I may live in a progressive society, but our parents remain old-fashioned when it comes to money and gender roles. And we are happy catering to their needs (and mine) in this manner.

Whose Money Is It Anyway?

I think women in general—whether they are the top earner or not—should be monitoring the household finances and know how the household income is getting allocated. I also think that it's practical for the breadwinning woman to take care of the big-ticket stuff like the mortgage while he covers the smaller bills like cable. When your finances become complex and you have children, it really helps to get a third party involved, like a certified financial planner, to make recommendations and help guide your financial choices (more details on this to come). A planner can also bridge any communication gaps you're struggling with . . . and even get your husband to feel that your money is, in fact, "our money"— something Tim grappled with early on in the relationship. He never wanted to come across as interested in my assets, fearing that he'd give me the impression that he was with me for my money. While that's sweet, the tricky reality is that my money is our money *to an extent*. And I don't want to be the only one in charge of making financial decisions. He used to feel as if it was my role to make all the big decisions since I make the bulk of the income, but as I told him, "I don't want to be the only one on this island of 'she makes more.' It's very lonely. We need to be a team." And I don't like being the one who initiates ideas like hiring a financial adviser. The way I see it, by giving him an out when it comes to participating in the financial decision making, he won't be able to blame himself if something goes terribly wrong with the finances. That's more pressure on me. Even though he'd prefer that I look into how much life insurance we need, for example, or how much house insurance we should buy, I want him to take ownership, too.

The old rules about money couldn't be more obsolete when it comes to defining "yours," "mine," and "ours." How much of your hard-earned money belongs to you alone? When men are the primary breadwinners, they consider it "my" money and that "I'm sharing my money with you," according to Brad Klontz. On the flip side, when women make more, we might see it as "our money" because we think about the partnership, but all too often we can also fall into the trap of doing the "our money" thing to soothe our husband's ego. Unfortunately, that's risky territory.

While it's important to look at the family as one economic unit and allocate resources accordingly, when the woman makes more, the "what's mine is ours" approach can backfire. Why? Because as women, we are givers. We instinctively enjoy taking care of those we love first and putting ourselves second. And when we make more—and we feel perhaps unworthy or guilty that we outearn our spouse—we may not make the best personal financial choices. In my own life, I find myself feeling guilty when I go shopping for clothes, compensating by making sure I buy a few items for Tim while I'm at it. I shouldn't feel ashamed; he's never said anything or acted in a way that would make me feel that way. Part of me just loves to shop, and I truly enjoy buying things for him.

But to be 100 percent honest, I'd say my guilt has a little bit to do with wanting to prove I'm not being selfish with my money . . . that what's mine is, in fact, "ours" and that I don't reserve splurging *only* on things for *me*. While buying a new pair of shoes, I'll throw in a sweater for him. The message? *We're a team and you're worth it.* The irony is that Tim could care less about new clothes. And that money could have sat in my savings account collecting interest, with no hurt feelings.

So, to what limit should a woman's money be shared as "ours" in a relationship? After all, we live longer than men and pay more for everything, from health care to dry cleaning to deodorant. When emotions lead to unnecessary commingling of finances, it can be a recipe for financial disaster.

SIX FUNDAMENTAL TIPS FOR KEEPING A LEVEL PLAYING FIELD

---

1. **Establish long-term priorities and short-term schedules.** If he wants to feel involved and on par with you financially, he needs to roll up his sleeves and commit to some of the dirty work like paying bills, balancing the budget, and paying attention to potential investments for your retirement accounts. First, make sure to get on the same financial page and agree to goals so that there's no miscommunication. Once you both have a clear picture of the finances, figure out together how you want to delegate money.

2. **Decide who will manage the bulk of the finances.** While every breadwinning woman would do well to monitor finances, that doesn't mean you have to manage it all, too. While neither of you may enjoy managing the family checkbook, it does make sense to delegate money management to the person who is more interested, better organized, or simply more frugal. Either way, both research and anecdotal evidence shows that couples have to make a decision, not

based on income or gender, about which one controls the finances and that whoever makes the financial decisions must consult with the other. Otherwise you risk turning your spouse off in more ways than one.

3. **Stay transparent online.** Online accounts, such as banking and bill paying (e.g., utilities, mortgage, cable), should be accessible by both you and your partner. This is useful in case of an emergency and to have a clear picture of your finances. Free websites like Mint.com can provide each member safe and easy access to financial accounts, allowing you to visually track your spending and debt. Sites like Manilla.com give you a way to see when bills are due and pay them (it provides access to see spending and debt but doesn't track the financials in the same way as Mint.com). You should also check in together once or twice a month so you're both in agreement with what's going on with your money. Keep a running list of all online account usernames and passwords, including—but not limited to—your family cell phone plan, utilities, mortgage, joint credit cards, brokerage accounts, and insurers. Store a hard copy in a fireproof lockbox in your home or in a safe deposit box, as well as on a website like Passpack.com or Clipperz.com, where you can securely store all your household passwords in one place for free. Even if your husband is the one who regularly handles the bills and accounts, make a habit of checking these accounts frequently to make sure they're in good standing. Tim and I have a Passpack.com account; we can access our account from any computer.

4. **Make decisions by committee.** That means asking for help from your man when you need it, agreeing to compromise, and admitting when you're in over your head. I do this *a lot* in my relationship. It's not easy for a breadwinning wife to admit her weaknesses or ask for help, but it's essential. It's enough just to call or text sometimes and say, "Hey, can we afford this? Should we buy this? Is it worth it? What do you think?" It's critical to admit when you don't know some-

thing. It allows your better half to have his voice heard—and, quite possibly, save your financial behind.

5. **Lose your possessiveness of your money, but don't apologize for your mani/pedis.** As a breadwinning woman, you have to be prepared to give up total control of all the financial decisions and a little bit of the lifestyle you feel you can afford (or deserve). As women bringing home more bacon, we have to understand that we are in a partnership. While we've accepted that "my money" is "our money" (to an extent), are we ready to really *experience* what that means? After all, it may mean downgrading a tad or, to put it nicely, making more economical trade-offs. I won't ask you to give up certain luxuries that you should be proud to afford, but you shouldn't be spending like you're single.

6. **Make his money matter.** If your income is covering a lot of the day-to-day costs of living, your income overshadows his. But if he's making even some money, it's still money that could go toward a vacation, college fund, new car, down payment on a house, or some other big-ticket item further down the road. Tim has to play catch-up with his retirement fund, so much of his money goes toward that for now. And he's the sole contributor to the 529 plan we have set up for our unborn children. These allocations from him not only take away the burden on me to fund *both* of our retirements, but it'll be very rewarding for him when our kids can say, Dad was able to send us to college. Small amounts collected over time add up.

How to Determine What's Yours, Mine, and Ours

Every relationship, but especially those in which she makes more, should aim for managing three main buckets: Yours, Mine, and Ours. How that breaks down and what that ultimately looks and feels like will be different for each couple. Most importantly you want to create a system where each person maintains some degree of financial autonomy while there is also some degree of joint accountability. I can tell you from my own relationship and from other married couples, this system allows for better communication, more transparency, and feeling that you're not just roommates with benefits.

For some, this may sound like a pretty obvious strategy. Who wouldn't want to maintain some financial independence in their marriage while achieving some financial togetherness? But occasionally I do meet couples, both those earning an equal amount of money and those with a large income gap, who choose to keep everything separate. They split costs down to the penny like roommates: two credit cards go down for the bill at dinner; they flip paying the mortgage each month; he pays for cable and she pays for Internet since they're the same price. No commingling whatsoever. Peek into their fridge and my guess is we'd find his and her jars of peanut butter.

I find this practice of "what's yours is yours" and "what's mine is mine" also common among couples who marry later in life. After years of being financially independent or, perhaps, fighting over money in a previous marriage, these couples may refrain from any financial commingling to avoid fights or to maintain full control of their money and assets.

Psychologically it may make sense to play fifty-fifty, but modern romance should still maintain a semblance of old-fashioned bookkeeping by having at least one shared account between partners. After all, our vows haven't changed much even after centuries of matrimony, specifically our promise to be able to trust one other. Why not trust each other with some of our money?

Notice I said *some*. There are some couples who insist on merging every penny together into one big pot (and we'll meet them in a moment), but I think the healthiest structure is to divide the earnings into three clear channels: what's yours, what's mine, and what's ours. With this financial framework you can set the stage for making healthier decisions with regard to affording the family's needs, as well addressing individual needs and wants. It's also a way to level the financial playing field, for him to feel like a financial provider, even if he's earning much less. And not to frighten you, but based on my experience reporting on financial infidelity—where one spouse hides purchases or racks up debt on a secret credit card—such "cheating" often stems from a lack of financial transparency and accountability to one another in the relationship. Shared account(s) leave less room for financial philandering.

The Three Buckets

Yours. After one of my corporate presentations one day on how to save and manage your money as a young adult, a married guy came up to me and said he was having a tough time agreeing on finances with his wife, who made more and "controlled all the decisions." She didn't let him spend any of his own money but bought herself stuff all the time. Fair? Turned out he had no independent savings account of his own. There was a "her" money bucket and a "their" money bucket but no "his" money bucket. I recommended that he establish his own financial spending account and that he consider using his money to cover longer-term savings goals for the family, such as paying for a vacation or the down payment on their next home.

No matter how much money the man makes, he needs his own financial autonomy. He also needs his own "slush fund" for personal purchases and emergencies that he should pay for by himself. Besides, how else will he be able to discreetly buy you gifts? Plan for him to carve out 10 to 15 percent of his paycheck every month into his own personal account. For the gentleman who came up to me that day, I think the stickier issue for him was his marriage to a controlling wife. I sensed he felt like a failure in terms of financial "contributions" since she seemed to pay all the bills and wield all the power. And he wasn't convinced he could hash it out with his wife. As relationship coach Alison Armstrong cautions, if either person assumes money equals power or a leg up in the relationship, you're in trouble. He was nonetheless encouraged by my advice and looked forward to taking my ideas home.

Mine. It is chiefly important for female breadwinners to maintain an account that is strictly hers for personal savings and/or spending (and takes into consideration the fact that she's likely to live longer and pay more for items in general due to gender price discrimination). Allocating up to 20 percent of her paycheck automatically each month into this account reserves her the freedom to enjoy her hard-earned money. It can also help minimize money fights; if you want to make a purchase, you can use this account without having to ask or get permission. Practically speaking, this money can also provide a financial safety net in case of an emergency or hostile separation. Since we know that when she makes more there is a greater chance for divorce, this money will be the key to her financial security.

Ours. This can be a shared account that pays for a joint goal, such as satisfying day-to-day family expenses or affording a big expense down the road, such as retirement. It can also include one joint credit card (no need for any more, really) that covers the family's needs and wants and is paid off in full, from either the joint account or just her account, since she is the main financial provider. Make sure that you decide on a "price threshold"—the amount above which any purchases that you or he wants to make are discussed beforehand. I suggest $100 or $200 as the minimum threshold for conversation. So if you want to buy a $200 printer for the household, using the joint checking account—and you're in the store considering the purchase—have a quick phone call or text chat about it. Maybe you decide to hold off until the two of you can do an online search after dinner or check the *Consumer Reports* rating.

Full Disclosure: Farnoosh's Financials

Here's how Tim and I manage our money. Our paychecks stay separate. They don't funnel into one big pot. Within our separate accounts we each maintain an adequate amount in checking to cover the monthly expenses we're each accountable for and in savings to stay financially independent. I maintain a separate credit card strictly for business-related expenses. And Tim maintains a separate credit card for his own discretionary purchases. Then we have a joint bank account that we opened up after getting married, in which we deposited some checks gifted to us. We plan to put that joint savings toward the down payment or closing costs on a new house. We also share one joint credit card for the majority of our day-to-day expenses, which I pay off in full every month (I also pay the mortgage). It's a helpful way to maximize points but, more important, it's a way to streamline many of our family-related purchases and stay organized. What we charge on this joint card constitutes roughly 80 percent of our family expenses. This includes some dinners out, groceries, vacations, gas, car maintenance, insurance, furniture, family gifts, household products, and the like. We also put the charges for Tim's evening software development courses and my certified financial planning class and textbook material on the joint credit card. After all, our individual education helps the well-being of our family. It's an investment in our futures and I'm more than happy and proud to be able to afford that for us. If our paychecks were reversed, I know Tim would do the same for me.

I also use this card for my own personal wants like clothing, manicures, and haircuts. Since I pay off this card with my own income, I feel it's okay to make personal purchases on it.

Tim pays for a lot of expenses—the other 20 percent—on his own with his personal credit or debit card. He'll pay for some dinners with his card when we're out with his family; his clothes; and his day-to-day incidentals like subway fare, cabs, haircuts, meals on the go, and a gym membership. He also pays for some of our utility bills, which he was already assuming prior to our marriage. (We lived together for a couple of years before getting married, when none of our finances were combined, with the exception of [and I admit, it's a biggie] a home we purchased together one year prior to getting married.) And frankly, I don't care enough about some of the utilities to take control of them. While I appreciate our cable service, for example, this is something Tim more enthusiastically researched and chose, so that's become his jurisdiction. He also pays our monthly garage fee, which is technically a "family-related" expense, but he began paying for it before we were married and we never made the switch. What can I say, some things are just left to convenience and old habits, and that's perfectly fine as long as there's mutual trust that no one's going to go off the rails and, say, default on the cable bill!

In terms of investments, we both contribute to various "family" investments from our own individual bank accounts. For example, as I mentioned, Tim funds the 529 college savings plan for our future child or children (because it's never too early!) and fully maximizes his 401(k) at work. Because of our income disparity and the fact that it's easier for me to cover most of our living expenses, we've decided that this is a smart way Tim can be a major financial provider for our family. His aggressive saving now will bolster our family's security later. I also invest in our long-term financial security by contributing to my own retirement accounts (which we will share one day, obviously), securing us life insurance, and buying myself a disability insurance policy in case I cannot work for a long stretch of time due to medical reasons.

While we fund separate individual retirement accounts, the assumption is that our savings will be mutually beneficial when it comes time to withdraw in retirement. In that way, even though we claim separate ownership of them, we consider them to be "our" accounts. With the help of a financial adviser, they remain transparent and we make sure each stays on track with annual contributions.

Finally, we share a taxable brokerage account with both our names on it. Our financial adviser makes recommendations and I fund this account from my own income as a supplement to our existing retirement accounts.

Note: if one spouse doesn't make any money, then there's presumably only one pot, "ours." The only exception here would be the need for an additional account if there's inheritance money or previous savings to keep separate.

A Sole Account for Better or Worse

In my research, I've found that the idea of marriage or sharing a religious faith often justifies couples' decisions to pool all their money together. They deposit their checks into one account and hold all savings and checking under both of their names. There's an immense level of trust and "togetherness" among these couples. "At the end of the day the money just has to go into the pot. The idea is that pot is what sustains this household no matter who is working. We don't quantify [the money] any other way," says Kelly, thirty-nine, a software manager and mother of two who earns twice as much as her husband, Brad, a manager at a wholesale and commercial paint distributor. Before they walked down the aisle in 2001, they consulted with a church minister (interestingly enough, it was her dad), who offered the couple some financial advice. "He explained to me from more of a marital counseling perspective that when you put your money in the same place, it shows a new level of commitment. Otherwise, I could just leave tomorrow with my chair, and he could leave with his TV. . . . But when you combine incomes, there's more at stake. You work harder to make it work."

I'm not one to get in the way of personal beliefs and approaches toward marriage, but I question whether couples are really being practical by combining everything. Corey Allan, a marriage therapist and devout Christian who runs SimpleMarriage.net, tells me that "a joint account can be easier and more 'open' when it comes to finances, but [it] can also be a source of contention." Rightfully so, Allan stresses the importance of communication before and during the relationship when it comes to deciding on types of accounts. "Each couple should play to their strengths and what's most practical for them," he recommends. "If they choose separate accounts, it's probably wise that each person have some level of access to the accounts." Allan and his wife started with a joint account then switched to separate accounts to remove some of the struggle between them about every penny that was spent and where. But they are both named on their individual accounts so in essence they are technically joint accounts while in practice they regard and respect them as separate accounts.

According to Allan, the main factor in all of this is the idea of "shared meanings." What money means to one person doesn't necessarily mean the same thing to the other. So the more you can understand the shared meanings involved, the less explosive this (and every other) subject can become.

On Twitter, I asked my followers whether they think it's wiser to have shared accounts. I asked: should dual-earning couples toss all their money into one big pot?

The reactions were mixed:

- Yes. I would hate for my husband to tell me that I can't spend "his" money.
- No. Too many couples don't agree about the decision-making big picture.
- Fund the 401(k) and the Roth IRA, pay the bills, put 10 percent in savings, then share the rest by having one account. No hiding, no divorce.
- Keeping his money and her money apart is a demonstration of a partnership, not a marriage.
- Yes. If you can't trust your spouse with finances, you should not be married.

If you can't figure out what's best for you, then let's take this lesson one step further and consider the emotional side of the equation, which is arguably a more critical factor than the how-tos of picking a payment strategy.

Payment Options Based on Your Emotions

If you're still wondering how to approach your bills despite the "yours," "mine," and "ours" allocation, then I do have some additional guidelines that can at least provide some parameters from which to decide whether to split everything, share designated bills, or rely solely on your income for daily expenses. This exercise looks at the "emotional audit" needed to ensure that you and your significant other stay happy. The psychological baggage you and your partner carry will play a much larger part in helping each of you to find your preferred role and feel comfortable in it.

♦ **Option 1: Big and little.** In this scenario, the major bread-winner pays for the larger expenses while the other partner covers the minor costs of living. For newlyweds Rebecca and Edward, for example, while they both paid an equal amount toward the down payment on their new home, she pays the monthly $3,000 mortgage, since she earns three times more than he does. Edward pays for other shared expenses within his means, such as the $500 monthly maintenance fee to the co-op building and the $100 monthly cable bill. Rebecca pays for most big-ticket purchases, such as plane tickets and vacations, but he covers the costs of vacation dinners and other outings on trips. She bought the car, but he pays for gas, insurance, repair work, and maintenance.

Best for: Couples where she makes much more and has more cash deposited in the bank to easily pay for large expenses, but he makes a decent salary as well. A "decent" salary here is defined as an income strong enough for him to cover the minor costs of living without strain.

Emotional audit: "Little" expenses—the monthly $30 payment to the online newspaper subscription and $100 check to the power company—can add up, and if he's saddled with picking up all the smaller bills, he may soon find himself strapped, stressed, and resentful. After all, it can feel emotionally taxing to make several payments a month compared to writing one big check. Make sure the sum of the smaller payments is tracked and discussed, and show your appreciation once in a while for his taking care of all those constant, small-scale expenses.

◆ **Option 2: Going dutch.** The trusty old fifty-fifty split rule many of us follow in casual social settings with a friend can also be applied to household matters with our loved one. However, it can be dicey unless your split is truly fair.

Best for: When she makes more, but not by much, or when she puts most of her bigger salary toward investments.

Emotional audit: Can he really handle paying for half when you make more than half of the income? "Men who make less than their wives but are forced to split the bills evenly may become secretly angry, and that anger is bound to emerge," writes Harriet Pappenheim in her book *For Richer or Poorer*. I agree with this observation. If splitting bills fifty-fifty starts to feel like a source of stress for either of you, consider pooling an equal percentage of your individual incomes into a shared account and use that to pay for joint expenses and activities. For example, let's say you net $90,000 per year while your husband takes home $80,000 after taxes. Now let's say you decide to pool together 80 percent of that after-tax income into your household account, which translates to $72,000 from you and $64,000 from him. Fair and square.

◆ **Option 3: Single-income savings.** The major breadwinner pays for almost everything in the living expenses department and the partner's income goes chiefly toward debt repayment, savings, or a personal account of his or her own. (This is different from option 1 because here the breadwinner covers *all* living expenses, including the smaller stuff like monthly subscriptions and utility bills.)

Best for: Couples where there is an immense income disparity. If couples are able to live on the wife's income, the money her husband brings in can go toward investments and his own fund for gifts and personal items. Marion, a thirty-two-year-old freelance writer from Utah, earns roughly five

times her husband's $30,000 a year salary as an adjunct profes-
sor. They've been married for ten years and she's always made
more. They make it work by using her salary to pay for their
lifestyle and his to pay back debt and invest in their future. "We
definitely couldn't maintain our current lifestyle on my husband's means," says Marion. "The disparity is too big." They
treat his income "like a windfall," socking it toward student
loans and retirement. That way, if he lost his income, they'd be
fine on hers alone.

Emotional audit: If the income you both are living off of is
solely yours, make sure to voice your concerns about any ex-
penditures and extravagances. Otherwise, it's natural to feel
like you're being taken advantage of, when in reality your husband may not understand how far your paycheck really
stretches. But be mindful of your man also feeling "kept" if
you're not showing immense appreciation for what he brings
to the table, be it an ongoing commitment to servicing the
debt, savings, and retirement accounts or just the support he
provides at home in partnership with you (emotionally and
practically speaking).

I cannot reiterate this last emotional audit point enough.
It's relatively easy to feel unappreciated, resentful, and taken
for granted—especially if you are footing the lion's share of the
expenses.

Trust and Responsibility

Unlike Kyle and Lily, whom we met at the beginning of the chapter,
Farah and Ahmad of Nevada have found a happy balance in their
relationship that would otherwise be very lopsided from a finan-

cial standpoint. They've leveled the playing field throughout their thirteen years of marriage, during which she began to outearn her husband by a long shot. Farah, thirty-eight, is making a little more than $200,000 a year as a rheumatologist while Ahmad, forty-three, earns roughly $80,000 as an IT specialist. He works partly from home to be able also to manage their three children (aged eleven, three, and two) and "play the soccer mom role."

When they first got together, Ahmad was the chief breadwinner, working for a Fortune 500 tech company while Farah was earning her medical degree and completing her residency. Her success is a deep source of pride for Ahmad, as he feels very much a part of it. He says, "For every woman who makes more, there's a guy behind her helping her make more and I've been helping [Farah] out." Originally from Pakistan, the couple has gone against the cultural norm since it's not common for the woman to make more in traditional Pakistani marriages. I sense that Pakistani and Persian mothers are alike in many ways, for during my interview I learned how hard their role reversal has been on Ahmad's mother, who visits for a few months every year to help out. At various times, Ahmad has heard his mother express disapproval under her breath, insinuating that Farah works too much, that their kids "need a mother," and that Farah isn't living up to her social duty of entertaining on weekends. In traditional Pakistani families, the wife typically throws big parties on the weekends for friends and family. But in this household, weekends are savored for quiet family time. (I was amused by Ahmad's confession that he cannot be strictly a stay-at-home dad with no professional responsibilities outside the home. He tried it once for a few months and admits, "It's a lot of work! I like to be with the kids for two to three hours max. The weekend is enough.")

Ahmad and Farah divide their household chores evenly, but he manages most of the money even though they don't have shared

financial accounts. He controls the savings and retirement accounts, including her 401(k) that he promises to grow to $1 million
by the time she turns fifty. And he has access to her online checking account so he can see the money move. While she pays for all
the big bills, including the mortgage, he covers bills that are no
more than $250 (e.g., utilities, electric, etc.). They each send money
to their parents back home every month, too. When I asked Ahmad about his take on the matter of "his money versus her money,"
he told me that while he does feel some ownership of her income,
he's more cautious and careful about spending it—much more so
than when he was the primary breadwinner. They rarely fight over
money and instead bicker occasionally about smaller issues, such
as her being late getting home to help with the kids, or leaving dirty
dishes in the sink overnight.

"There's a lot of trust in the relationship," Ahmad said. He went
on to say he and his wife are well aware that things could be different. He could make more money if they wanted, but that would
come with a cost: being close to their kids. Ahmad sees his role as
a father as one of great responsibility. And he offers a good example: "We have a friend in his midforties who just for the first time
saw his fourteen-year-old son's soccer game. He lives in a two-
million-dollar house, but if you can't see your kid's soccer game, it's
not worth it."

Indeed, trust and an individual sense of responsibility in whatever
role you're playing provide a strong foundation to any relationship.
But these will only get you so far. You might think you have all
of your financial dealings figured out, and then something unexpected happens, which Rule #3 doesn't cover. For example, what
if he wants to support his ailing mother financially and you are
the chief breadwinner? What if he has to pay alimony and doesn't

earn enough, but you do? What if, upon entering the marriage, he has substantial credit card debt or student loans? Are those your responsibility to pay off? What about gifts he wants to give to his friends or family members and that cost more than, say, $50? And what about the dreaded "nup" question: should you consider a pre-nup or postnup? Put simply, how do you buy yourself freedom and peace of mind when you know there are a lot of wild cards in life?

This is when you'll need Rule #4.

RULE #3 RECAP

- In marriages where the wife brings home a bigger pay-check, the woman is twice as likely as her husband to make all the financial decisions, which isn't a good idea in general.

- To keep a man's dignity and sense of engagement, he needs to feel that he plays an important role in the relationship and that he's not completely isolated from the financial decisions. This requires that you level the financial playing field, a two-part process of figuring out how to pay for living expenses big and small and how to manage the emotional challenges that come with the financial disparity.

- Before figuring out the "mine," "yours," and "ours" division of financial accountability, be sure you're tuned in to your ingrained thoughts about money and to how your upbringing has affected how you deal with money today.

- Although it's fine for him to manage the bulk of the bill paying and investing if he's better at all that than you (or simply has more time and prefers this role), women who make more should stay acutely attuned to the financials and know how the income is being allocated.

CHAPTER 4

Rule #4: Hack the Hypotheticals

Financial decision making and planning are not always clear-cut, as there are a lot of hypotheticals to navigate, or "hack," with a trusty strategy. The ailing in-law. The money-sucking alimony bills. The debt he amassed years before you met. His college roommate who wants a personal loan to start a business. The expensive toy he "must have." How do you address these thorny issues?

First, some general questions you should always ask yourself when you're at a crossroads and can't figure out whether or not you can afford something for the relationship, but from *your* paycheck:

- If the paychecks were reversed, what would I expect from him? What would *he* do? Put yourself in his situation and see what kinds of emotions and empathy emerge.
- How might this affect the stability of my own future if I outlive him? We know that women need more money in general for their futures since they are more likely to

live longer and will have to pay for everything if and
when they lose their spouse. So you can't base financial
choices just on whether he would do the same for you.

- Even though this is something for him, am I neglecting
  to see how this is also something for us?
- Money doesn't always result in happiness, but would
  paying for this thing we're contemplating make our
  lives easier or better in the long run?
- Where does this fall on our hierarchy of goals? Can we
  easily afford it? This may be a function of where you are
  in your life—what stage you're living in and the attending responsibilities, obligations, and risks (financial,
  health, or otherwise).

Now, let's get to those hypotheticals, starting with the agreement that's supposed to prepare for the biggest hypothetical of
all—a breakup. If you're in a relationship headed for marriage, is a
prenup a good idea? And if you're already hitched, should you get
a postnup?

Don't Pooh-Pooh the Pre- or Postnup

"The angriest person in any divorce is a woman who is ordered to
pay spousal support." So says divorce attorney Lee S. Rosen of
North Carolina. He's been in the business for more than twenty-
five years and has witnessed the trend of women making more over
the past decade in particular. Although it was unusual ten years
ago for him to see cases where the woman made more, today he
sees a steady flow of them, and he senses from his experience that
a higher-earning wife can be a "recipe for disaster in a marriage"

(although he admits that he's only seeing the marriages that don't work out). But he doesn't see as many prenups as he'd like when he's dealing with divorces among couples in which she makes more. And he's not asked to write many of them for such couples about to walk down the aisle. He thinks this is because women just don't think about them like men do. "The guys are very paranoid about protecting themselves financially," he told me. But he thinks, unsurprisingly, that it's smart to get one. "I think it would be crazy for a woman who makes more not to have one," he asserted. "A prenup is the only sure thing you can do to protect yourself." He points to the higher odds of getting a divorce when the woman makes more and adds that it's possibly less difficult to negotiate when the woman makes more because guys are hesitant to accept that they'll need help in the event of divorce. Hence, a man would be more willing to sign a prenup. (Interestingly, Rosen also thinks that high-earning women don't contemplate the chances of divorce in the same way men do. According to Rosen, marriage is more about romance than anything else for women. And he's probably right, but I'll add that we women probably contemplate the chances of divorce differently from men regardless of our income. Nonetheless, we should smarten up a little more and be more realistic, planning for those what-ifs despite being distracted by our romantic intentions.)

In 2011, the American Academy of Matrimonial Lawyers (AAML) found that the number of prenups had jumped 73 percent over a five-year period. Although women are indeed asking for them in record numbers today, it's still a relatively small percentage compared to the number of marriages taking place—most people don't have prenup agreements. I hope to see this change. With couples getting married later in life, and young women earning more and buying property faster than men, there's simply more at stake. Divorce court is no longer about angry wives filing for alimony and child support. More women are finding themselves paying their former husbands alimony and child support than ever before. According to the AAML, 56 percent of divorce lawyers across the country have seen an increase in mothers paying child support in the last several years. What's more, 47 percent have also noted an increase in the number of women paying alimony. In Rosen's experience, he's never had a case where the woman feels it's justified that her husband receives support. I think that speaks volumes about what we women should be doing to protect ourselves.

Rosen confirmed my hunch about the most common complaints he deals with when he's working on a divorce between two people and the woman makes more: the lazy husband who sort of has a job but isn't trying very hard to generate more income or who is "self-employed" as a fledgling entrepreneur, sales rep, or real estate agent but not really working. He sees this scenario time after time. And the longer the woman has to support her lackadaisical husband, the quicker her feelings of frustration move into the bitter zone, after which the resentment takes over. What I found most intriguing in my interview with Rosen is that there seems to be a clear difference in how men and women cast blame on their marriage's demise. Rosen says the biggest accusation from dependent husbands is infidelity, yet these men don't necessarily want the marriage to end—it's the women who are initiating. And while some of these women do indeed cheat, in many cases their reasons are purely emotional.

As it turns out, in fact, women walk away from marriages two-thirds more often than men, which is true across all marriages no matter who is bringing home the bigger paycheck. But the reasons for doing so aren't what you might think. It's not so much because the women wake up one day and realize they no longer love their husbands or that they've grown apart and no longer share the same values or lifestyle. In an article for the *Huffington Post*, journalist

Vicki Larson brings up a lot of interesting context for who initiates divorce today and why. She references a National Marriage Project study (formerly at Rutgers University, now at the University of Virginia) that implies women are not afraid to ask for divorce because they know that the kids will likely stay with them. The nature of divorce laws in most states favor a woman receiving custody of her children, so "men lose *a lot* in divorce"—not just money but also their kids. The Marriage Project study also points out that "the higher rate of women initiators is probably due to the fact that men are more likely to be 'badly behaved.' Husbands, for example, are more likely than wives to have problems with drinking, drug abuse, and infidelity."

When I asked Rosen for his advice to women who earn more, other than just getting a prenup, he stressed the importance of keeping a close eye on the finances and having access to the money. He sees cases where the wife earns more but has little to no time to manage the finances. So she lets her spouse take over and doesn't even have access. And when it comes to divorce, that can put you in a really bad bind in the short term as you have to suddenly pay for emergency housing and attorney fees. The lesson: if you sense the relationship is not going to last, it may be smart to sit down with a divorce attorney and discuss your postnup options. And you want to do this privately.

I spoke with other divorce attorneys on the matter of pre- and postnuptials, and all agreed that it's ideal to consider these documents seriously if you're making more—especially if you "find it necessary to rewrite your state's divorce laws," in the words of Jon Gallo, an attorney I introduced in chapter 2. He and his wife, Eileen, run Gallo Consulting, a financial and estate planning firm in California. For example, Gallo says, if you get divorced in California, a "community property" state, without a prenup, you may be held to that state's "fifty-fifty" divorce laws, which say couples must split assets, including savings, property, and even debt acquired during the marriage. (Community property states include Arizona, California, Idaho, Louisiana, Nevada, New Mexico, Texas, Washington, and Wisconsin.) Most states, on the other hand, are "equitable distribution" states where a judge takes into account countless criteria to determine who gets what. Divorce coach Deborah Moskovitch, author of *The Smart Divorce*, makes a living helping others to navigate divorce so it's not as legally complex, emotionally nightmarish, and costly as usual. She, too, values the power of a prenup, which she views as divorce insurance that's not just for the megarich. Although it's an unsexy conversation to have because it could imply that you don't trust your partner, Moskovitch essentially tells people to take the emotion out of the conversation and regard it as just an adult way of thinking about finances. I tell women that the best way to make this less unpleasant is to just be up-front about the fact that it's not about love or trust or lack thereof. It's simply a smart way to protect each of your futures from a purely financial standpoint.

Something else to keep in mind: if you anticipate a large inheritance or business earnings during your marriage that you prefer to keep separate, pass down to your children from a previous marriage, or walk away with in the event of a divorce, establishing a prenup may be necessary to avoid conflict and court proceedings.

How you want to manage sentimental assets like heirloom jewelry and other valuable inherited items should also be outlined in a prenup. And while a home acquired prior to the marriage by one of you doesn't automatically become "shared" property in the eyes of the law, if you both begin contributing to that mortgage, one could argue that it's now a commingled asset. In that case, a prenup stating that your house is your house even if your spouse makes contributions to the mortgage could protect you against any argument that he's entitled to a portion of the equity when you split.

And don't just evaluate your current assets when considering the benefits of a prenuptial agreement. If you're an ambitious woman (and I assume you are if you're reading this book) and have high hopes to start your own business or grow an existing business in the next several years, a prenuptial agreement can also address the what-ifs. What if you sell your business for $20 million? What if you inherit $5 million or a beach house from a long-lost uncle? Anticipating your own successes is a critical step in planning and drafting prenups.

Even if you just choose to live together without getting married, and both contribute to a mortgage belonging to just one of you, the home can become shared property in some states. If you break up, a court could decide you both technically own the house, in which case you might have to bring in a lawyer to help settle the dispute over the property.

Next door in Canada, too, a prenup may prove essential for couples who simply choose to live together. That's because the provinces (minus Quebec) recently passed a law that grants common-law partners the same basic rights as married couples after two years of cohabitation. For example, couples who've shacked up together for two or more years are eligible for a fifty-fifty split of shared debts and assets, excluding any prerelationship property or inheritances. Remember Chelsea, the forty-five-year-old TV producer and writer from Toronto? She recently broke up with a beau because she was worried he'd inherit 50 percent of her condo after living together and him contributing to the mortgage. "He wanted to move in with me . . . and I said, 'You need to sign a prenup,' but he refused and that killed the relationship."

Some things to be aware of: a prenup cannot dictate child support (though it can state how often the in-laws get to visit!). Child support payments are determined by state guidelines. And once you sign the prenup, you are allowed to update it with the help of an attorney. Various alimony reform laws are currently in different stages of passing around the country, so a financially independent woman has no choice but to be vigilant. Know what's going on in your state, and hire professionals who have their fingers on the pulse of the latest developments so they can accurately analyze all implications for your financial future. Ask about things like alimony and child support laws in your state and how they can, or cannot, be spelled out in your agreement. You don't want to be targeted later by a mad ex-husband who tries to get money from you to support his kids from a previous marriage.

The process of creating a prenup or postnup will vary depending on the complexity of your circumstances (and of course the hourly rate of your attorney). They can cost as little as $1,000 or more than $10,000. A final note about these documents comes from Moskovitch: whether you've got a prenup or a postnup, make sure there's an element of fairness. Otherwise it is more likely to be contested.

Have a Plan for Handling Individual Debt

This is a topic for debate. The very practical and rational side of me believes we should keep our personal debts separate in marriage. But love sometimes finds its way to conquer all—even debt, when it probably shouldn't.

On the one hand: If you are concerned about your spouse's personal debt and want nothing to do with it—and I don't blame you—you must be mindful and keep close track of how that debt gets resolved. Your spouse's personal debt brought into a marriage—as long as it doesn't bear your name—is not your liability. (Note: There's a big misconception out there that says debt brought into the marriage becomes shared legally. Not true; only the debt that bears your name is yours. Even if a spouse acquires a loan during the marriage—without cosignatures—the liability belongs solely to that spouse. The *only* exception, which still needs a judge's decision, is if, say, one spouse takes out a loan during the marriage that "serves the interests of the marriage" and the couple lives in a community property state. In a divorce, the court could order that both parties are responsible for it. And, of course, if you share any accounts with your spouse and he falls behind on debt payments and collectors come after him, they could dip into a joint account . . . and therefore affect both of your finances.)

Be careful that your spouse doesn't fold that debt into, for instance, a shared home equity line of credit or transfer it to a joint credit card. In those cases, even if he vows to be solely responsible, realize that you've technically still inherited his debt and are equally responsible in the eyes of the law. If your husband has a lot of personal debt, best to maintain separate credit accounts. Check your credit report annually to make sure you recognize all the credit and loan accounts stated under your name (you can visit AnnualCredit Report.com to download a free report per year from each of the three major credit-reporting agencies).

On the other hand: I do know of high-earning women who've willingly paid off their husbands' student loans or credit card debts so that they could, together, establish a "clean financial slate" and qualify for such things as a low interest rate on a joint mortgage or joint car loan. If you're less worried about the size of his debt and more concerned that his personal financial setbacks are preventing the both of you from achieving your goals, then you'll have to think long and hard about whether or not you want to contribute to that debt and put your own finances on the line. A family friend once told me how she paid off her husband's $10,000 credit card balance when they initially got married so that they could qualify for a big-

ger mortgage together. While I nearly passed out when she told me
this, I realized this was a very personal decision and it did offer
some benefits. The two were able to qualify for a mortgage and buy
a beautiful home a few years later.

FARNOOSH'S DEBT COMPROMISE

Here's a strategy that helps to resolve an individual's debt
with both of you pitching in. If your husband enters the marriage with debt, whether it's a few thousand in credit card
debt or tens of thousands in student loans, give yourselves a
timeline, maybe six months, maybe two years, during which
time you, the primary breadwinner, take over many of the
day-to-day expenses and saving responsibilities. He, on the
other hand, uses the majority of his paycheck to wipe out his
debt on his own. If he makes $50,000 in take-home pay, then
he should put as much as he can—75 percent, 80 percent, 90
percent—toward that debt. Even if we're talking six-figure
loans he'll be out of debt within a few years at that rate. You
effectively become the "provider" while he does "damage
control." Consider it an investment in your relationship.

Why is this strategy better than just writing a personal
check from your bank account to his Sallie Mae or American
Express account? There are several reasons. One, you don't
feel like you're "bailing" him out. You don't ever commingle
the debt. And he goes through the pains of the debt payoff
process—with no quick fix from his breadwinning wife. As
someone who's been in debt, I know it's important to experience the lesson of paying off every penny on your own. It
deters you from getting in over your head again.

Set Ground Rules for Gifts

This protects both you and him. It takes the pressure off him to buy extravagant items that you can afford and he can't. But it also takes the pressure off you to "provide" by showering him with gifts. As a team, establish ground rules for gift giving. Perhaps it's a set amount, such as $50 for friends and $100 for family birthdays. Or challenge yourselves to spend nothing and let the gift focus on free events or excursions, not purchased items. Replace the idea of buying a gadget with spending a day at the beach, at a museum without an admission fee, or on a hike and picnic. This way you manage expectations and no one feels bad for spending more or less than the other.

AVOID A BLUE CHRISTMAS

The holidays can aggravate negative underlying emotions. Growing up, I witnessed Persian husbands shower their wives (often in front of others) with jewelry, cars, and various other bling. The rational side of my brain understands that was all for show. But my irrational side—the one that sometimes clouds my judgment—wishes I could be that adorned wife sometimes, at least on Christmas. So to manage expectations and reduce the focus on materialism during the holidays, we finally decided to put an end to exchanging big gifts. Now we just do stocking stuffers, or occasionally we'll take a winter weekend getaway. You, too, might have to set similar limitations for yourself to avoid the negative feelings that accompany a time of year filled with inevitable extra stress and expectations. Santa probably won't bring your hubby a financial windfall so think about buying a gift for yourself.

Take Care of Aging Parents Carefully

What if he wants to support his ailing parents financially and you are the chief breadwinner?

As a married person you must accept that you've inherited a family that's much larger than just you and him and your children. Often in-laws must also be taken into special account. I'm of the camp that says my parents should not get any more or less special treatment than Tim's parents. We are all one big family and if someone needs our financial help, then it's at least worth having a detailed discussion. If your husband wants to help out a parent with, say, medical expenses or nursing care, the discussion should encompass all the ways—financial and other—that you may be able to assist this relative. The conversation should also involve other siblings and how as a family you may all be able to help Mom or Dad.

If you anticipate needing to help either of your parents financially, start a separate account for "future" emergencies. Literally budget for it, as you would your children's college education. If for some reason your husband wants to give more than what's been allocated for this financial emergency, then in that case, he may have to figure out a way to come up with the money on his own. If the account has $5,000 and he wants to give $15,000, then he should try to come up with the extra $10,000 out of his own slush fund. And what about sudden, life-threatening illnesses that come out of the blue on either your or your husband's side of the family? Then I say it doesn't matter whose money it is—you should try your best as a couple to support the sick member of your family. Even my own financial planner—married with two kids—admitted to putting her house on the market to come up with the money to pay for her mother's unexpected cancer treatment. The only reason she ended up keeping her home, she explained, was due to the fact that her mother passed away all too soon.

Involve your parents in this financial planning and approach them about their plans and preparedness for old age. This may help to avoid the need for any emergency financial assistance. Here are six more tips:

Act soon. Even if your parents are healthy, time is of the essence. The sooner you can have an open discussion with them, the sooner they can start mapping out their goals and actually seeing them through. Talking about money is not a simple conversation no matter whether you're twenty-five or sixty-five. But it has to happen. If a parent is ill or disabled, there's even more reason to engage with them as soon as possible.

Don't give up. As parents, they may not want to get into details about how they manage their money or how much they have in savings. I won't sugarcoat it: it can be awkward. But be the bigger person and if you feel resistance from Mom or Dad or both, first understand that their hesitance may simply be rooted in some old-fashioned sensibilities. They could very well want and need your assistance but are too shy or proud to admit it. But whether they realize it, their aging does potentially impact you in more ways than one. My friend Michael, a small-business owner, wasn't exactly successful when he initially approached his parents for the Big Talk. Looking back he realizes his approach wasn't ideal, considering his parents held their finances pretty close to their chests. "I was clumsy and started the conversation about [what they were planning to do with] their house. They looked at me like I was insane. 'We're going to live in it' was the response I got. When I pushed they got defensive. I backed off. It took a couple of different starts like that." Ultimately they let him into their world, thanks to never giving up.

Tap siblings. You may want to consult with a sibling or a close relative to help you break the ice with your parents. Of course, you don't want to stage any sort of intervention or broach the subject over Thanksgiving dinner, but rather come together as a unit, a team, to express your love, interest, and support. It may help to use anecdotes of other aging loved ones who may not have had the best retirement plans or executed wills and kept their children in the dark to get them to really understand the gravity of the matter.

Get organized. The AARP recommends gathering the following key financial information from your parents ahead of any possible emergency:

- Bank accounts and passwords
- Contact information for their financial professionals like accountants, attorneys, and brokers
- List of current monthly bills and how to pay them
- Insurance policies
- Tax returns
- Credit reports
- Medical records and doctor contact information
- Estate planning documents and the location of their will

Let them continue running the ship. Remember, Mom and Dad are still the adults in the picture. While they may eventually overcome the challenges of opening up to you about their finances, it's very important that you help them still feel in control of their choices. Your role should be to primarily ask a lot of questions, present hypothetical circumstances like a disability or medical setback and not dictate to them what to do. Parents should feel ownership of their decisions. As my friend Michael reminds me, parents excel at telling their kids what to do—no matter their age.

Access free resources. When in doubt, don't underestimate the power and help from third parties.

Sites like AARP Money Management Program (www.aarpmmp

.org) and the National Council on Aging (www.ncoa.org) can offer some direction and guidelines for how to best communicate and plan with your parents. And of course, if your parents work with any attorneys, insurance agents, or financial advisers, you should loop them in and see if they have any recommendations, as well.

Don't Forget About Life and Disability Insurance Policies

As the primary breadwinner, you'll need a bigger policy than he will, but don't discount the size of his policy since you'll likely live longer. And while disability insurance is important for both of you to buy, it's essential for you since the family's finances are more at stake if you cannot work. Tim and I hacked this when we first got married, hooking up with an insurance agent who helped us qualify for various policies. The life insurance part was simple enough, but for me, as a freelance writer, attaining disability insurance was quite challenging. Of the six or seven insurance companies that considered my case, only one offered to insure me. Like many freelance journalists and writers I'm considered a "high-risk" client not only because I travel occasionally for work but because of the sheer nature of my job, which is that I write. Apparently insurance companies fear that a writer could cry writer's block in a frivolous claim. The lesson: Cast a wide net when shopping for policies since every insurance agency has different underwriting rules. Use a broker who's well versed in these policies and the various insurance companies. Don't give up!

Get Professional Help When Planning for the Future

Financial planning for the future is one area where couples should seriously consider asking for help. If your husband says he'd like to manage the retirement account and college savings funds, fine. But make sure he really enjoys it and is *excellent* at it. Otherwise, a financial professional is a must. Your husband may take your squabbles over securities too personally.

To find a certified financial planner (CFP): First ask around for referrals from friends, coworkers, and family members. Get some background on each recommendation to make sure the person is in good standing with the CFP Board (the Certified Financial Planner Board of Standards; at www.CFP.net); you can also check out discipline records there. The websites of organizations like the National Association of Personal Financial Advisors (www.NAPFA.org) and the Financial Planning Association (www.FPAnet.org) can help you learn more about CFPs in your area. A planner who is a *fiduciary*, who vows to act in your best interest, is an absolute must. Consider fee-based planners who charge a percentage of your assets under management, usually 1 to 2 percent, depending on the size of your assets (the higher, the smaller the fee). Other planners work on a commission basis, meaning they earn a cut of the revenue when they sell you a particular financial product, like a mutual fund or annuity. This isn't my favorite kind of planner since this incentive may cloud their objectivity and duty to act on *your* best interest alone.

To find a certified public accountant (CPA): As with finding a CFP, ask around for referrals first and make sure the names on your list all come with the CPA designation. According to Accountant.org, a database of accounting professionals, it will run you an average of $25 to $50 an hour to work with a CPA for minimal bookkeeping. For further help, like tax and investment planning and execution, fees can range from $150 to $400 per hour depending on the nature and scope of your situation. One way to reduce your costs is to opt to work with a staffer a bit lower on the totem pole than the manager or founder. It also cuts down on your time and money to attend meetings prepared with your short- and long-term goals, along with a tally of your monthly income and spending. To locate a CPA near you check out the National Society of Accountants (www.nsacct.org) and the American Institute of CPAs (www.aicpa.org).

RULE #4 RECAP

◆ When dealing with unexpected expenses or something you're unsure you can afford (e.g., buying an extravagant item, covering your mother-in-law's medical bills, or giving your sister money to fund her start-up company), first ask yourself what your husband would do if the roles were reversed. But do so while keeping in mind that you will likely live longer and might need that money, particularly if it's a very large expense.

◆ Every breadwinning woman would do well to consider a prenup or postnup.

◆ Have a plan to deal with debt that preexisted the relationship. There's no one-size-fits-all formula, but you need a compromise that's fair and equitable. If you can't reach an agreement on this matter, seek professional help.

◆ Set monetary ground rules for gifts, including the gifts you and your partner exchange and gifts you give others—children, family members, and friends.

◆ Be prepared for and careful about how you will help take care of aging parents and in-laws. If you can, start the

conversation with your partner about this thorny area
long before a parent or in-law becomes sick or incapacitated.

♦ Buy life and disability insurance when you can, and don't
hesitate to hire a professional for help in planning your
future through the expertise of a CPA and/or CFP.

CHAPTER 5

Rule #5: Cater to the Male Brain

Leveling the financial playing field is actually a multipart process. Once you've figured out the logistics of money management, there's plenty of work to be done in handling the emotional ups and downs of adapting to this new economic reality, which can aggravate your inner selfhood. Feelings of resentment, as I've already noted, are inevitable, and many breadwinning women who are holding down serious, well-paying jobs identify strongly with their careers and professional responsibilities. Our sense of self tends to struggle when thrown into a relationship that entails certain compromises and sacrifices. I'm all too familiar with how the income disparity itself plays out in terms of valuing and respecting each other's work—and "work" is a loaded word. Some occupations with some cachet that come with a low paycheck (e.g., teacher, firefighter, paramedic, carpenter) get a societal pass, whereas other jobs (e.g., part-time barista, stay-at-home dad, truck driver, personal trainer, retail clerk) can be easy to undermine. And "work" can sometimes mean something totally different from a job that pays. It can be the work of taking care of kids, cleaning the house, doing the laundry, or just being there to support our withering selves after a long, hard day.

As breadwinning women, we want to feel proud about our partner's accomplishments, no matter how much money he makes. Having a partner with a less-than-stellar career can be awkward in certain situations, if not agonizing. This is true whether you're dealing with personal interactions with your partner alone or those that entail others (family, friends, colleagues, and strangers). How can a high-level actuary stay blissfully married to a bus driver for more than twenty-five years? You're about to find out and glean insights on how a woman in the financial driver's seat can preserve not only her own ego but that of her man. It's critical to value what a man contributes to the relationship even if the money earned isn't equal. By the same token, salary does not equal ambition. As a woman who makes more, it can be really tough to separate work from your relationship and even more challenging to remember that your partner also has stress related to his job.

Which is why it's key that you level the *emotional* playing field through a simple strategy: cater to the male brain. This is Rule #5.

There's no denying the fact that time really does make a huge difference. The longer you know someone, the easier it usually is to get along, understand each other's needs and how to show appreciation, learn how to cater to one another's line of thinking, and make minor adjustments along the way so your relationship—and family life—work better. Time is what helped Ryan, forty-eight, and his wife, Julia, forty-six, achieve a healthy rhythm in their marriage of twenty-one years, despite the astonishing differences in their income and the types of jobs they each fulfill. Ryan is a school bus driver who makes about $11,000 a year while Julia banks $92,000 as a pension actuary. Although Ryan used to have a higher-paying job working for a power equipment company, his wife has always made at least double his salary. They waited eight years to have kids, during which time they really got to know one another and hit a comfortable stride. He became Mr. Mom when their son entered first grade, and he then started to drive the bus when their daughter became a kindergartener. When the kids were young, he constantly fielded questions from his male peers like "When are you going back to work?" And when he explained that he was a full-time parent, many would reply, "Oh, you're babysitting?" Today, now that the kids are older, he still gets heat from friends and old colleagues who continue to ask when he's going to return to work.

Luckily, Ryan and Julia have never had power struggles related to their income disparities. They pool their money together and since he's the better bookkeeper, he takes care of the bill paying and investing. It no doubt helps that while they are different in most other ways, they are both frugal savers. During their childless years when they were both working full-time, they managed to pay off their mortgage. And over the more than twenty years he's earned less than Julia, he's become more comfortable with himself, only wishing society were kinder to his chosen work. At times he has felt "inadequate" in the sense that he lacks a skill set to earn the kind of income Julia makes. But he reminds himself that he's got one of the most treasured skill sets around today for relationships in which the woman earns more: the ability to make certain sacrifices to support the family in ways besides money. And he's not the type of guy who needs his ego stroked all the time. Ryan has a strong sense of self and what he brings to the table. "All jobs have value," he says. "Oftentimes the dollar value doesn't equal the reward value."

How true that is. It's what I wish every couple would remember, for it can help us navigate not only tricky financial terrain but also the emotional aspects. How we view the exchanges and trade-offs we make in our relationships factors mightily into their dynamics and whether or not we succeed in them. Unfortunately, not all of us are in relationships that work as seamlessly as Ryan and Julia's model union. If there's one thing that Ryan and Julia can teach us, it's that making a relationship work in which she makes more is, more than anything, about doing what's best for you despite social norms and customs. But this, as we all know, can be hard. It's why Rule #5 is an essential tool. As women, we live inside our own heads all day long, which can think quite differently from a man's. With a little insight into the male brain, we can learn how to avoid those power struggles, stay acutely attuned to his feelings of self-worth, and all the while get what we need from our partner to be happy.

Men Thrive as "Providers"

Relationship coach Alison Armstrong, whom I introduced in chapter 1, has studied men (and how women relate to them) for the better part of her life. She's famous for teaching women how to properly interpret the signals we may receive from our men and how to deeply connect with them. These signals have to do with the ways in which we can nurture healthy egos despite the imbalance in our gender roles and honor the inborn power divides between men and women to promote a gratifying partnership. After transforming the lives of thousands of couples through her workshops, including many relationships where the woman holds the financial card, she has proof that men love strong, competent women.

According to Armstrong, and as I mentioned briefly in the first chapter, it's the "What do I need you for?" attitude women often can have that keeps men at a distance and can be destructive in a relationship. Interestingly, Armstrong believes that we women have inherited an adversarial relationship with men today; we say things to them—knowingly or unknowingly—that can bring out the worst in them and can potentially rupture their sense of self-worth. Among the many ways we can emasculate men is by criticizing, complaining, taking over a task they're perfectly capable of performing, correcting them, interrupting them when they talk, or letting them know that they've failed (which, if you didn't notice, are acts that will piss most of us women off, too, if we're the recipients!). At the same time, we cling to the false idea that we can change men. We can't, and we shouldn't even try. Instead, Armstrong inspires women to treat men as they are designed to be: successful providers. While the *financial* provider in a partnership can most definitely be the woman, that doesn't mean the man cannot contribute in other ways that are equally valuable. "He will thrive as a provider if what he does [financially speaking or otherwise] is what you authentically regard as the most important thing [in your relationship]."

Don't let your sense of entitlement get in the way of showing your appreciation.

One of the first things Armstrong pointed out to me is that as women, we often make the mistake of thinking that the "veto" goes with the money. In other words, whoever makes the money has the power to say no and call the shots. But Armstrong says that's a highly hazardous and mistaken way of thinking, especially when the tables are turned and a breadwinning woman suddenly thinks she holds the reins. "Women [in traditional relationships] put up with men vetoing because they make the money. But men veto for different reasons than women. They veto the things that they perceive as a threat to whatever they're protecting. He'll veto going to the movies on a Friday night, for example, because he's protecting his energy, he's tired. He'll veto the pool in the backyard because it's an unnecessary expense that will ultimately hurt the retirement fund. If a woman thinks that the power should follow the money, she's in deep trouble. She won't be able to help her husband at all because it'll be a power play and nothing will work." To this end, Armstrong offers some advice: "A breadwinning woman has to first figure out what she thinks her making more money gives her the right to and what she deserves. She's got to look at what she thinks it means that she makes more money." I think that's excellent advice. We need to get our own priorities and expectations straight in our heads first before we enforce them on our partners.

Avoid Financial Mommying

Sometimes it's not so easy for breadwinning women to trust their men, especially if the men have had some financial missteps and have yet to prove they can be financially responsible. As one husband put it, "The biggest thing that I would consider emasculating to me is being in a position where I am trying to check out at a store and having trouble getting in touch with my wife . . . and I have to wait to hear back from her that it's okay to buy a Coke and a candy bar."

That's what Mason, thirty-eight, says about his sometimes unsatisfying life. His wife, Ashley, thirty-five, handles all the finances in their marriage, including the amount of money that goes into his checking account. Mason pretty much gets a small allowance each week, enough for incidentals and gas. "We had an incident where basically a bill didn't get paid [by Mason] and at the same time he overdrew his account with his debit card so suddenly his account was $700 in the red," recounts Ashley. "And I kind of lost my mind a little bit because that's a whole lot of money."

"I have impulse problems. I'm terrible with money," Mason concurs. "I'm incredibly terrified of fucking it all up."

Their current financial setup seems to be feeding the beast, namely, Mason's lack of financial confidence. Ashley's financial "mommying," for lack of a better term, is problematic for her as well. She doesn't enjoy assuming all the power or feeling unable to trust Mason—feeling more like a parent than a partner. "For me the struggle is to not feel like his mom. Like, being entirely responsible for the finances really contributed to that sort of 'mean mom' feeling because I was always saying, 'No, we can't do that because we have to do XYZ,'" she says.

The solution? Mason needs to make more money and build up his savings, and the two of them need to have his and her accounts that they fund themselves, along with a shared account for common purchases.

Speak Directly to the Male Brain

Armstrong's work is all about partnership, which she admits is messy and constantly working itself out. If a higher-earning woman thinks money is the most important thing, then empowering her husband is going to be really tricky because the underlying message from her is the fact that her man isn't doing the most important thing—making more money. And men want to do just that: the most important thing. That's what being masculine is about. He will thrive as a provider if what he does is authentically regarded as the most important thing by the woman, even if that "thing" isn't bringing home the bulk of the income.

"Accountability" is a big, important word in Armstrong's vocabulary. In her view, we need to ask men to be *accountable*, not necessarily "helpful." In her own marriage, Armstrong wants her husband to do the grocery shopping not because it will help her out but because he takes it on as his job. He's accountable for making sure the family has dinner and fresh food in the home. "This distinction really helps," she says. So, according to Armstrong, you need to ask yourself: what do you need your partner to be accountable for—what can he provide—that allows you to say you're absolutely better off with him than without him no matter how much money anyone is making? Of course, the million-dollar question is how do we get our men to see it as accountability rather than "helping" us out?

Where many women go wrong is not sitting down with their man and doing what Armstrong calls "a Great Ask." This is when you state plainly to your man what you need, what it would look like, and what it would provide for you. And this is how you can allow him to take on being accountable for certain things rather than him just being a helping hand. When a man finds out, for example, that taking out the trash is something important to you and that he'll get appreciated for doing it without being asked, it becomes an easy thing to do. It becomes something he can feel accountable for, and it's not resisted. It's a way to win with you. This goes back to Armstrong's idea that men only want to do what really matters to their women. In fact, she is a firm believer that we can change our men's behavior just by coming from a place of appreciation and clarity rather than criticism. This makes sense, for it's much easier to be motivated to do things if we're going to be more valued and loved—not berated. But as women we tend to forget this subtlety in our exchanges with men. Armstrong thinks this happens because we ourselves are more motivated by staying out of trouble and by avoiding criticism, so we then try to motivate our men the way we're motivated. It doesn't work. When we nitpick and disparage our men in the hopes of getting them to do something, they just keep their distance. And, as we'll see in the next chapter, this plays into how we expect and encourage them to help out with housework.

The Big Three

If there's one reality that every breadwinning woman has to live with daily, it's the triumvirate forces of sex, money, and power. It's practically cliché to say that money equates with power, but it's so true that you can't evade it no matter how hard you try. And it's the eight ball in this kind of alliance. Money affects how each of you feels about one another and about your relationship, and it also directly influences the frequency of and satisfaction with your sex life. In chapter 3 I urged a breadwinning woman to step down as family CFO and learn to surrender some of the financial decision making, even if relenting in this area is against her nature. I realize that's much easier said than done, but of all the ego-boosting gifts you can give your man, this is perhaps the most effective one.

Brad Klontz claims that not including a man in financial decisions can have a "gelding" effect on his sexuality, making him essentially feel like a castrated version of himself. Even men who prefer not to be involved should at least be asked and encouraged to participate—just as you'd prefer if you were the dependent and your man was the breadwinner. Ultimately, if you earn more and you make the bulk of the financial decisions and do most of the planning, it can affect your sex life for both of you. In addition to wounding your man emotionally, it can affect how much you respect him and are even attracted to him (not to mention whether you feel like it's your duty to take care of his sexual needs as well as his financial ones). One breadwinning woman hit this concept on the head (literally) when she sounded off in *New York* magazine, saying, "I'm not going to pay the bills . . . and then come home and suck his dick."

It helps to understand that men incorporate money into their identity in a way women don't. We might be hesitant to measure our job satisfaction or overall success by how big our paycheck is, but men aren't. And because of that, it affects a man's self-esteem and confidence if his salary isn't as high as his partner's. For this reason alone, eliminating men from financial decisions undercuts their self-worth and can even make a husband feel emasculated. According to Kristy Archuleta, assistant professor of family studies and human services at Kansas State University, men who make less don't even realize that they may feel threatened by or jealous of their wife earning more. She says: "The jealousy is displayed through other behaviors like needing to control things (distancing himself emotionally, trying to prove his worth by working more hours or buying expensive things, or bits of sarcasm: 'That's a nice purse. Can we still pay the mortgage next month?'). [It can even result in] depression and anxiety."

Which begs the question: how do we avoid nudging our partners out of too many financial decisions? After all, we can't let him become a yes-man—someone who always gives a thumbs-up to us, perhaps at the expense of his own needs and wishes. That's not the definition of being a real partner. You can't be fully engaged in a relationship if you're just nodding your head the entire time. And that can really weigh on a person's ego, man or woman. My breadwinning friend Dana, who's blissfully married to Kurt, gave me some great marital advice before I took the plunge: "Always ask your husband for his advice, even if you know the answer. If he doesn't give you the answer you want, discuss it. Even if you still get your way, he'll feel like he was heard and that's critical." Other women I've interviewed have offered similar advice. Ask for his input regardless. Even when you know you can handle a certain challenge at work or in your personal life, bring your man into the conversation so he feels needed. There's nothing worse to a man than feeling unessential and whose ideas and thoughts aren't respected. Remember, think about this from the other side: if he was the main breadwinner and constantly left *you* out of the loop, you'd eventually feel unworthy, unappreciated, and even unloved. This scenario cuts both ways, so be aware of it.

Relationship expert Marni Battista also agrees that asking for help (even when you don't really need it) is essential. She often reminds her top-earning female clients to play up their "sexy alpha female" or to "fit in the feminine" in their relationships so that, in turn, men can feel masculine and take the money thing off the table. This further involves being comfortable with chivalrous gestures like letting him open doors for you and give you his jacket when it's cold outside. This isn't as simple as it sounds and not so easy for some of her clients, Battista finds, since women sometimes falsely correlate being feminine with being weak. "There is an epidemic in the lack of women stepping into their femininity, even though they are breadwinners or more successful financially," she observes. When I ask her why she thinks that is so, she tells me that some women harbor beliefs that, "If I ask for help, then I'm weak, and weak is bad. It connects back to being vulnerable."

Is there a way to get over this? According to Battista, "If you have a hard time letting him help you or be chivalrous, that's something you need to work on [because] it's an easy way to make a man feel masculine." She suggests to women a trick she calls the Costanza, taken from a *Seinfeld* episode in which George Costanza "does the opposite" of his instincts. "If he says, 'Can I give you my jacket?' Say

'Yes.' Stand there and let him open the door . . . You have to suck it up and be uncomfortable. It takes practice," she says.

Every relationship is a two-way street. But, dare I suggest, when a woman makes more she must step up to the plate in ways that society never prepared her for. Put simply, she must work harder at the relationship and pay much more attention to her man's self-image than women whose incomes are smaller than their husbands'. Sorry, ladies. I know this may not seem fair. But it's the game we've chosen to play as the top earners. Trade-offs exist in all that we do, but nowhere are the trade-offs as hugely sensitive or challenging than in a relationship where the woman is the main income generator. The dynamic taps innumerable issues—from our sense of pride to our ability to respect and love another human being.

Stroke It, Stroke It, Stroke It to Death?

All of this brings up another good question. We know men have egos (let's forget about ours for the moment). And historically, his paycheck and ability to provide for his wife and family fed that ego. In relationships where she makes more, should it be a woman's responsibility to stroke her partner's ego regularly so he doesn't feel bad? While women need to be sensitive to his plight and carefully navigate the potential minefields inherent in this disparity, shouldn't men be encouraged to buck up and face this new social revolution head-on? What can we expect of men at this point and where should women draw the line and say, "It's not my job to make you feel better about yourself!"

To address this quandary, I turned again to Kristy Archuleta, whom I deeply respect for the breadth of wisdom she brings to the table as both a researcher and a practitioner. As a licensed marriage and family therapist in private practice who also conducts financial counseling and therapy in both private and public settings, she hears a lot of stories and sees a lot of patterns in the people she meets. I know she agrees with me on the need to stroke a man's ego when he earns less, but how much is too much? When does the stroking morph to dangerous mollycoddling?

Like any well-respected academic, Archuleta was quick to admit that "the answers are not one size fits all." But she then offered her professional opinion from a highly practical standpoint that's worth noting. The idea that men who earn less need their egos specially stroked "is something that husbands need to come to terms with and then be up-front and honest about it in the relationship so the couple can work on it together."

Beware of the double whammy: the need for an ego stroke is *itself* an issue of self-esteem to contend with that can create conflict in a relationship. A man making less demands more attention to his ego, but be careful about that attention turning into mothering. We can unintentionally mother men in an attempt to stroke their ego. Kavita J. Patel, a New York–based "love coach" who has worked one on one with hundreds of women to reclaim their love lives, including executives at Google, Amazon, and Microsoft, warns women about this very problem. Men are not wired to receive compliments and gestures of caretaking the way women are, which is why overly copious praise or "mommying" will subvert your good intentions. She says, "If you are treating him like a child— even if he does make more and you start to mother him or coddle him in certain ways—then we can get so wrapped up in that, we come off as condescending and emasculating." The problem worsens when the woman feels like she needs to stroke his ego constantly and feelings of frustration and bitterness bubble up under the surface. No sooner does this vicious cycle commence than frustration erupts on both sides of the relationship and a widening chasm develops. What's more, this distance won't take place in just money matters; it will leak into other areas of the relationship, such as each person's role related to household duties, parenting, and sex. Patel offers another sage piece of advice for catering to the male brain: "Ask for what he *thinks* [about something], not what he feels." There's a subtle but powerful difference here, for men in general are not as in touch with feelings as they are with thinking. He's more likely to respond much better to *What do you think about this?* rather than *What do you feel about this?*

I wish there were a one-size-fits-all answer to the question of how much is too much, but the number one takeaway I've learned in my own experience working with couples and speaking to experts is that in addition to respecting a man's way of thinking, every couple can choose the way in which they make financial decisions, so long as the man is involved to some degree. I covered this matter briefly in chapter 3 but it bears repeating because it has everything to do with tending to a man's ego. Regardless of which payment option you choose, even if you know who will pay for what, the logistics of budgeting, allocating assets, and managing bills should be a shared endeavor. It doesn't have to be an equal split, but the bigger the income disparity, the greater the need to have the man's input on financial decisions if just to honor his self-identity as a contributing member of your team.

Do What Works for You, Period

Although past research has shown that major decisions often lie with the person who makes the most money and that the wife (presumably in a traditional role) is likely to make financial decisions related to the household, more recent research reveals that the best way to make financial decisions is to do what works for you as a couple. In other words, if the wife chooses to make the decisions about investments while the man is keen on managing a home renovation and writing those checks (or vice versa), then that is what makes that particular couple happy. So instead of wondering how men can become more involved in decision making to nourish his ego, the question should be how couples can become more satisfied in their relationship in regard to financial decision making. Those in fulfilling marriages say they do what works for them—period. It's not a matter of who makes what; it's not based on gender or income. Once a couple has established the parameters for who covers which bills based on the mathematics of each person's income, the rest is about balancing out the power of financial decision making based on who *wants* to take charge of what.

And let me add that if you and your man do, in fact, decide that you'll take on most of the spending and bill paying with your money as the chief breadwinner, make sure to initiate access. In other words, invite your husband to view your accounts. I mentioned this on page 64: stay transparent online. This is not just a way of saying "I love and trust you." It's actually critical in the event that you are—God forbid—injured or sick and cannot pay your bills. Your husband can step in and move money around. Even if you are automating many of your payments (and I hope you are), it's important to give him the keys to your financial life, which is very much *his*, too.

"The irony is that, if you think about biology and evolution, the culture has changed faster than the animal brain has. In terms of breeding, men feel the need to be the alpha in order to be an attractive man. Women's purpose is to reproduce. Society and our prefrontal cortex have evolved but our lower animal brain tucked behind the outer cortex is stuck on the

thought of 'What does this mean for my status?'" —Brad
Klontz

Find Your Rhythm and Mind
Your "Man-Hers"

By and large, the thorniest road to negotiate of all is the one inside
our own heads. We are born with built-in technology—physical
and emotional—based on our sex. That's not going to change.
What's also not going to change anytime soon is the animal brain
seated squarely in each of us that dictates certain behaviors. While
still debated in scientific and anthropological circles, many assert
that women biologically want to connect with an alpha male much
in the way a man seeks an attractive, compliant female with whom
to procreate (or "spread his sperm," as the biology textbooks often
say). When those roles are reversed and not given consideration in
the relationship, a man can feel devalued and the woman will share
that belief. This is when the guy will try to look for validation in
other places and perhaps entertain an extramarital affair. A breadwinning woman, on the other hand, may also stray, only to find
herself with another beta male, under the misconception that he's
not going to leave her.

Brad Klontz has some strong opinions on how a couple can
mind their inner mammal that yearns to keep traditional gender
roles, well, traditional. He'll be the first to state boldly that many of
the decisions we make as men and women are *unconscious*. While
it may sound shallow to say that we'll lose our attraction to our
partners when gender roles are severely reversed, it's just the plain
facts of life. Our lower brain, the part of us where we harbor all of
our primitive drives, including those for food, water, and sex, just

can't handle the twenty-first-century's role reversal. It's not equipped with an upgrade to its technology that commands emotions and behaviors—even when those knee-jerk reactions doom the relationship, as is the case with an affair.

So how can you protect your relationship given the high risk of divorce when you make more? First, and this should sound familiar, start by looking at your family as a single economic unit. Don't focus on who makes more or less. Families that do really well respect the total income as "our money" rather than viewing one person's and the other person's separate money as income "to share." Granted, this is more about mind-set than anything else. Often the couples who have the hardest time with a role reversal are those whose incomes were fairly equal until the man lost his job. And if that couple identifies more with traditional roles, only to find themselves thrown into a very different kind of relationship dynamic, then they are at most risk for divorce. This is when two choices must be considered: (1) challenge the mind-set or (2) encourage the guy to make more money. This may necessitate some professional counseling.

Second, understand that financial and emotional equanimity are moving targets in any relationship, especially one of this high-stakes nature. If you don't love your position, change it! "Figuring out a balance so that neither of us resents the other is a work in progress," writes one blogger who makes twice what her man does. "And I suspect it always will be, actually. We don't really have social models—or a definition of successful, positive masculinity—to lean on in this kind of scenario, no matter how common it is and no matter how much [my significant other] and I look at each other and say it just *shouldn't* matter." But we all know that it does matter.

When new circumstances call for a rethinking of your payment strategies, return to the drawing board. Be willing to experiment and make shifts as you go. And when arguments arise, see if you can take a thirty-minute time-out before engaging in dialogue. This gives you time to reflect and process your feelings. You'll come to terms with the emotions that are bothering you and then be able to ask for what you want and need from your partner. For me, writing is cathartic; I organize my mind on paper when I'm mad or frustrated (usually after I've let off some steam cleaning my kitchen or rearranging shoes in the closet) so I can really understand what I'm feeling before I say something I don't mean or will later regret.

Earlier I noted how large surveys have revealed that many women admit to being uncomfortable earning more. And as one expert put it, a woman's financial dependence on a man "has lost none of its attractions." Again, we have our innate drives based on our sex to blame for this confusing set of emotions, needs, and wants despite the roles we want to fulfill today. A breadwinning woman's DNA doesn't want to be the alpha in a relationship, yet we're forcing ourselves to be just that—and as a result we're fomenting a war within our lower brain that's aching for us to maintain habits dating back to the days of hunting cavemen and gathering cavewomen. To some degree, we're all hunting and gathering today but doing so with an old set of tools. If we can at least admit (no matter how politically incorrect it may sound) that we're genetically wired to rely on men, we can better manage the role reversal and all the mixed expectations. Awareness alone will help us make headway with actually thriving in this new economic order.

I've covered a lot of territory in Rules #3, 4, and 5 from both an economic and an emotional standpoint. But several other aspects to making a marriage under these circumstances work remain— practical issues like managing household chores and day-to-day living responsibilities. Who takes care of all that? Small business owner Katherine solved this problem when her kids were young.

On the brink one fine day, she asked herself, "What's it going to take for me to not do one thing in this house?" That soon led to hiring a housekeeper once a week. It's a costly expense but for her it's the difference between happiness and misery. Katherine confesses that she doesn't know if she would still be married if she hadn't hired a regular housekeeper. "At first my husband protested the idea, but it's a nonnegotiable," she told me. She's learned over time that expecting her husband to do all of the housework is just ridiculous and managing it herself is out of the question, given her workload. She picks her battles carefully. "It irritates me that he leaves his dishes everywhere and throws dirty clothes on the floor in the laundry room . . . but I would never say a word to him about it." City dwellers, the couple also spend money on take-out food and prepared meals delivered at their doorstep several nights a week.

Which brings us to the next hurdle to clear in mapping out a game plan if you're a breadwinning woman: getting everything done on the home front and keeping everyone happy. I call it Rule #6: buy yourself a wife.

RULE #5 RECAP

- ◆ In leveling the emotional playing field, it helps to acknowledge and appreciate what each of you brings to the table, financial or otherwise.
- ◆ If, by virtue of your breadwinning role, you're making the rules for spending and saving, be sure to avoid coming across as dictatorial. Be as democratic as possible, avoid financial mommying, and never equate income power with having the ultimate authority in the relationship. Include your partner in financial decision making. The overall power must be shared.
- ◆ Figure out what you think your money gives you the

right to, and what you deserve, before you ask for that from your partner.

◆ In catering to the male brain, understanding how men think differently and what motivates their behavior (or lack of action) will go a long way to help you communicate successfully with them to get what you need while stroking their ego, ever so delicately, in healthy ways.

CHAPTER 6

Rule #6: Buy Yourself a Wife (and Other Tips to Avoid Domestic Drudgery)

If you have a demanding career and are pulling down a significant income, then why are you coming home stressed out about what to cook for dinner and finding time to clean the house? Unfortunately, a lot of us have inherited the idea that we should avoid spending money on things we can do ourselves or that are otherwise expensive and seem extravagant to outsource. So we feel guilty when we pay for a housekeeper, get takeout, or pick any other shortcut that makes domestic life easier but comes with a price tag.

Sadly, too many women are trying to do too much. As you know by now, studies show that the more money the wife earns, the more housework she does compared to her husband! But here's the real stinker: when women outearn their spouses, they are often stuck doing the worst kind of housework. The men coach baseball, buy groceries, and mow lawns while the women change diapers, scrub toilets, and wash floors. This pattern persists in developed nations around the world. In a study of thirty-two countries, men were always less likely to do laundry, which is still considered to be among the most labor-intensive jobs. The gender gap in both housework and child care only narrowed when it came to pleasant, discretionary tasks that took the least time.

Moreover, kids seem to make the "motherload" worse. Couples with kids tend to share chores less equitably, even though there are typically more chores to tackle. A recent study in Norway and Sweden (countries that often set the benchmark for being progressive on the gender equity front) found that having children reduced the odds that a young couple would report equal sharing by 27 percent.

No wonder housework has been called the last feminist frontier. Progress on balancing the chore chart has apparently stalled. For all the advances we've achieved in the workforce, the traditions of domestic life have been slower to change. And get this: A 2008 U.S. study revealed that every $1,000 a woman earns translates to an extra $17 to pay for cleaning, laundry, and eating out. By comparison, the same increase in a man's salary means only an additional $9 for those domestic duty shortcuts. In other words, women's salaries often pay for "women's work."

While men are carrying more of a domestic workload than in the past, they still don't take on nearly as much as we do at home. And this, as you know, is ground zero for many people who argue and become hostile to one another over household duties. Conflicts about cooking and cleaning are a significant source of stress in families. But unlike, say, monthly bills, chores are everyday responsibilities. You have to get them done, and they don't go away on their own.

(At the current rate, Oxford University sociologists suggest that we're only halfway through what they see as an eighty-year transformation, which means it will take until 2050 for a truly equal gender division of tasks. Yikes!)

According to psychiatrists Harriet Pappenheim and Ginny Graves, one reason we take on more housework in addition to working a job outside the home is that we feel the need to compensate for our success in the work world by covering traditional wifely roles at home. (And as I noted in the first chapter, researchers have suggested that the wife whose success seems "threatening" to her husband takes on a greater share of housework so as to assuage his potential unease with the situation. The wife, of course, may ultimately get tired of working this "second shift," which may be one of the explanations behind the higher rates of divorce among such couples.) Or, the psychiatrists speculate, a husband whose masculinity has been rocked by his lower income feels that pitching in around the house would be the ultimate blow to his manliness. Meanwhile, some men have become used to being mothered by women and assume that "women's work" at home is still just that.

Regardless of what's fueling this behavior, when a woman makes more, she needs to find a way to dial back housekeeping duties so she doesn't burn out. As many sociologists and economists have noted from a broader standpoint, we best not find ourselves sparring over who takes out the trash or who gets to scrub the toilets. And a breadwinning woman cannot be expected to cook, clean, and pick up his socks—all ingredients for negative feelings, including resentment.

In the 1960s, Nobel Prize–winning economist Gary S. Becker pointed out that when a woman knows the bulk of child care and housework will be on her plate, she'll likely make different choices about her career and how much time she'll devote to it. There are legitimate reasons why women choose teaching over doctoring or engineering (and this is true for women of the past and present). She's also more likely to step off the corporate ladder when she has kids. But the laundry should not be one of her reasons for doing so. And it has been a motive for generations of women before us today.

This fact is partly why Sheryl Sandberg extolls the virtues of finding a husband who will get his hands dirty in the kitchen and bathroom. It's also why a 2010 article titled "Housework Is an Academic Issue" argued that universities could improve the research outcomes of female professors by adding allowances for domestic help to benefits packages.

Now a professor at the University of Chicago, Becker argues, as a recent article in Canada's *Globe and Mail* puts it, that "the division of labour still comes down to two forces: earning power and what he calls 'productivity'—that is, personal decisions around which parent wants to be home, or who is most able to handle the chores." So, much like how you manage the finances in the relationship, the person who's the best at housework or gravitates more naturally toward it is usually the person who will inherit the bulk of the responsibilities. Is that fair? Of course not. But the goal of managing your housework is not about finding a rigorously fair and square fifty-fifty resolution with your mate. It's about optimizing through the use of your collective strengths, inclinations, and means.

See It His Way First

Nancy is a perfect example of someone who has let her husband's lack of domestic effort really get to her. A banker in her midthirties who makes six figures working and living in Manhattan, Nancy is the sole breadwinner in her relationship. Her husband of six years, Mike, has been trying to get his own business off the ground for the past year and a half but he hasn't turned a profit yet.

One of her biggest gripes is that her husband has no interest in keeping their apartment clean. He believes domestic drudgery might as well be her domain since, as she explained it to me, "I'm the most OCD about it." Nancy assured me that his perspective doesn't stem from cultural or gender expectations; he's just rationalized it in his head that since she's so obsessive about cleanliness, she should naturally be the one to figure out a strategy. And since she's not prepared to do laundry and scrub toilets after working twelve hours, she's gotten a housekeeper to come to their apartment twice a month. But it's not good enough. Her husband works from home and leaves dishes in the sink and clothes on the floor, and it drives her mad. So his solution? "Let's just have the cleaning lady come every week!" To which Nancy replies, "Oh, yeah, because money grows on trees?"

In all honesty, Mike is probably so focused on his business that he just doesn't care right now about the household chores or who does them. His whole life revolves around his work because he really does want to prove to himself (and to Nancy) that he can be successful. But this has come at a huge emotional cost to Nancy, who is exceedingly frustrated and lonely. After inviting me to a yoga class one night after work, she talked to me about her ambivalence about the marriage—not knowing whether she should stay with him or she'd be better off by herself. This, as Alison Armstrong warns, is dangerous territory. Once a woman begins to contemplate being "better off" alone, things can turn sour very quickly.

But Armstrong also teaches that sometimes we don't understand how our men think when it comes to household chores and multitasking. Men are, in her words, "single focused." Their brains filter things like dirty dishes in the sink as irrelevant. Cleaning only becomes important if they understand what it provides for someone else, she explains. Hence, if Mike's mind is centered on his work, he probably isn't prompted to act on the mess. Thinking about the different ways men and women tend to shop offers another way of understanding this. They hunt down exactly what they want, while women tend to browse.

This disconnect between the sexes is what fuels the arguments on the domestic front. When Nancy and Mike bicker over house-hold chores, they are miscommunicating their needs and misinter-preting each other's signals. Nancy thinks that Mike's hands-off approach means he doesn't care to listen to her and that he's not respecting her values. Mike, however, just doesn't care about housework. When she tells him that he's not "contributing," he of course assumes she means financially, when in fact she doesn't. Nancy is exasperated by the ongoing arguments and doesn't feel it's fair for her to pay for a cleaning lady four times a month with her money. Nancy's story got juicier the further I probed. I found out that they keep all their finances separate and that she pays for pretty much everything, which is probably fueling Nancy's feelings that he's not pulling his weight in the relationship. Mike only has small savings at this point, and she's given him two years to start making a financial contribution. Ideally, she told him, he should aim to make as much as (if not more than) her so that if and when they have kids someday, she can choose to switch to a less intensive career path. (She currently works seven a.m. to seven p.m.) Al-though she doesn't plan to stop working, she'd like the option to slow down for a little. She's honest with herself: "I can't keep going at this pace and have kids and continue to support my husband."

This has really blown Mike's self-esteem, according to Nancy. He's nervous that he won't be able to meet her expectations, and while she partly regrets throwing him a deadline, she admits that she needs to be realistic. Incidentally, she's seen several women around her at work who have gotten divorced at the point in their marriage when they were making more and subsequently were left to raise their kids with no extra financial support whatsoever from their ex-husbands aside from child support. Nancy has no doubt been influenced by these colleagues' experiences and the scary possibility that if divorce is in her future, paying alimony to him could be, too.

My advice to Nancy was to set up a shared account for the things she thinks are necessary to outsource for the well-being of her household unit. Mike must accept that a clean house is critical to the happiness of the household, but if he doesn't want to do any heavy lifting, then he needs to at least help get that part of their domestic life taken care of. I encouraged Nancy to have him contribute to the joint account even if it means dipping into his savings so that together they can afford a housecleaner, because it's something they both need.

Which brings me to an important lesson: don't enable his apparent laziness on the household front by outsourcing chores and using just your hard-earned money to pay for it! A clean house is everyone's responsibility. Nancy added quite matter-of-factly, "His behavior towards the chores isn't nice. It isn't fair. I know it's not how he would treat a roommate. So why would you treat your wife like that?"

While this is a good point, it's important for Nancy to learn how to speak to Mike in a way that hits home for him (see Rule #5). Armstrong would definitely have something to say about how Nancy communicates her needs and confronts the issue of housework. If she takes the criticism out of her pleas, she just might get more of what she wants. "[Most men don't] know how much an orderly environment contributes to a woman's sense of well-being and her ability to love and express and experience joy," Armstrong says. According to her, a woman will end up doing housework so that her environment is quiet, allowing her to relax. If she's tired but there are socks on the floor, for instance, she has to put them away first. And that's where the resentment comes in. But the truth is he just might not understand that you can't relax until certain things are tidy. And he probably doesn't know that the payoff of picking those items up is that you can finally be at ease—available, talkative, maybe even in the mood for sex.

Our need to be in a clutter-free environment, much more so than most men, might actually have some biological underpinnings. In 2013, the University of California Press published *Fast-Forward Family: Home, Work, and Relationships in Middle-Class America*, which reveals the results of a landmark ten-year study done by UCLA's Sloan Center on Everyday Lives of Families (CELF) looking at clutter and hormones. They found that living in a cluttered home can lead to considerable psychological stress for both men and women. The researchers measured stress hormones in participants' saliva, concluding that living in a messy environment is a bigger problem than previously thought, especially for women. Linguistic data gathered in the study revealed that busy working moms often talk about their houses with the words "chaotic," "messy," and "cramped," coupled with the words "usually," "always," and "constantly." These same women also showed increased signs of stress and a depressed mood as the day progressed. Men, on the other hand, reported little to nothing about the clutter or mess in their lives.

Such results are not a surprise to me. And neither was the statement put forth by Tamar Kremer-Sadlik, the director of research at CELF and coeditor of the study: "[Women] have been socialized to care more about the home—our identity is much more tied to how the home appears. That's why we make our lives harder by insisting that certain things have to be done in a certain way. We have to relinquish control. We can't expect everybody to do their share and still be the ones who decide who is going to get it done."

As much as my mom stressed the importance of bringing home straight A's, she also taught me to be a fastidious cleaner. I was just four years old when she put me in charge of loading the dishwasher after dinner every night. I remember her yelling at me once for placing the forks incorrectly and my dad telling her to ease up on me. "She has to learn," my mother snapped back. And did I ever. My chores growing up included cleaning the bathroom, clearing the dinner table, hand washing dishes that couldn't go into the dishwasher, and never leaving for school without a tidy bedroom and made bed. (My husband jokes when I follow him around the house with Windex.) My younger brother, on the other hand, didn't exactly receive the same pressure-filled domestic education as I did. Once, when he was twenty-one, he came to visit my house, and he asked where he should toss our dirty dishrags. I told him, "Just place them in the hamper in our room," to which he replied, "What's a hamper?"

Celebrated marriage counselor and author of the national bestseller *What Could He Be Thinking?* Michael Gurian, whom we met in chapter 2, also has some strong opinions about the division of household labor. In his view, if the woman thinks that successful partnerships hinge on whether he does enough housework, then she is going to fail in probably 70 to 80 percent of cases. He agrees with Armstrong: Men don't pick up the cues from women. They are inherently more spatial—they visualize the world around them differently than we do. And that's just who they are. (To clarify: men are better than we are at rotating pictures of 3-D objects in their heads whereas we are more likely to spot which of a group of objects has been moved to a new position. This biological discrepancy between the sexes helps explain why we each have our shortcomings when trying to tackle certain chores that are geared more for the male or, conversely, female brain.)

I see this in my own husband. It takes Tim much longer than me to pack a suitcase or clean off his desk at home. And when we designate an afternoon to clean together, I manage to tackle far more than he does in the same period of time. On more than one occasion Tim has turned to me, absolutely stunned, and said, "Wow, how do you clean so fast? You're really good at it."

So it follows, then, that if we make doing housework a nonnegotiable in our relationships, we're setting ourselves up for failure. We need to, in Gurian's words, "hire someone and get it off the table and then really look at how [we] can be equal as women and men—not as women projecting a standard on men, or vice versa." Clearly, the resentment will grow if he doesn't do his part in her eyes. "Listen to him on what his part is," says Gurian. "Men are actually able to come to the table and find and give equality."

Indeed, men can bring a lot to the household table even if it's not in the form of a dish towel, dustpan, and vacuum cleaner. Just because they aren't scrubbing toilets and dusting doesn't mean they aren't contributing in other ways, be they financial or emotional—points I've already made in previous chapters but which bear repeating. And as women we would probably benefit in many ways if we totally removed the household chore tug-of-war from our relationships. But if they won't lift a finger in this realm, then just be sure they lift a financial finger to some degree. After all, the entire point of a truly equal partnership is that you don't have to spend time arguing over who does what, when, for how long, and how well.

As in so many other couples, I'm the neat freak while my husband can work in a messy environment. My biggest pet peeves are a disheveled kitchen and unmade bed. I love to shred paper; he doesn't like throwing anything out. I make sure the rooms in our home are clutter free, but he ensures the car is serviced and kept clean. Admittedly, we don't cook often. But when we do, we split the task—I'll cook and he'll clean. We have a housekeeper who comes every two weeks. When we got married, I'd already been living in New York City for ten years and had gotten used to having a service help keep my apartment in good shape. He wouldn't have thought of hiring someone for this before marrying me, but it was a nonnegotiable (that we could afford, luckily) from the beginning.

What If You Can't Afford the Housecleaner?

It's a fair question, regardless of your income. A breadwinner who needs to put most if not all of her extra income toward something else in her life, such as her kids' education or medical bills, is going to be cornered. What is she supposed to do? Here are five strategies to consider.

♦ **Differentiate between a dirty house and a messy house.** A dirty house means food-stained dishes piled in the sink, a layer of dust on the curtains, and cookie crumbs in bed. This calls for heavy-duty cleaning, which is the sort that takes immediate priority. A messy house, on the other hand, means clutter and some disarray, and it doesn't require you to drop everything at that moment to clean—and later, feel resentful about it. It can wait.

♦ **Set a cleaning time limit.** When you do commit to cleaning—either just by yourself or with your spouse—set a timer. I do this all the time. Racing against the clock actually pushes me to try to get more done.

♦ **Pinpoint the small messes that might ruin your day and take care of them before bed.** In her book *The Happiness Project*, author Gretchen Rubin describes her "evening tidy-up" ritual, which involves putting a few things in order—filing papers, placing newspapers in the recycling bin, cleaning up the kitchen—before going to bed. Those are small steps that can help totally lift her mood in the morning. As she researched her book on inspiring happiness, she found that making the bed was "the number one most impactful change that people brought up over and over." According to Charles Duhigg, author of *The Power of Habit*, making your bed every morning is associated with better productivity and stronger skills at sticking with a budget. It has also been suggested that it can even boost happiness. Go figure. For me, the little things I like to take care of before bed include clearing dishes from the sink, wiping down the kitchen counter, and tidying up the living room.

♦ **Hire a teenager.** At fifteen I could have made a load of money cleaning other people's messes. The earnings would have put my babysitting money to shame. Chances are there's a young person in your neighborhood who'd be willing to help clean out your garage or organize your closets at home for a much lower fee than a professional maid service. Ask your neighbors. Post Help Wanted signs on trees and at your local high school message board. If you're a city dweller who lives in an apartment building, co-op, or condo, there's probably a teenager just a few walls away from you. Post a sign in your building's community area or mailbox room.

♦ **Enroll him in whatever you're doing and don't get nitpicky.** According to love coach Kavita J. Patel, she sees "too many women wanting household chores done in a specific way and wanting him to do this or that exactly the way she does it. If you're going to be in that space, you are putting too much pressure on yourself, and you're never going to get out of it. You have to let go of some things and ask yourself why it bothers you so much." She recommends that women "enroll" their men. So if you're doing the dishes, say "I will rinse them, you put them in the dishwasher," or vice versa. Men like to be enrolled in and understand the things that you're doing. Let him in on the details while you're going through it (e.g., "I use this soap because I like to do it this way" or "I use this kind of sponge for these types of pots," and so forth).

They're willing to learn; they're just not willing to be told what to do and have you be condescending about it. And they don't want to feel like they're doing it wrong all the time.

Attention, Parents: Don't Confuse Shared Housework with Shared Parenting

Marc and Amy Vachon are the founders of EquallySharedParenting .com, a website that helps couples achieve just that. They are also the authors of the book by the same name, *Equally Shared Parenting: Rewriting the Rules for a New Generation of Parents*. In it, they write that "the soul of equally shared parenting is not focused too heavily on equal housework," and they bring up a lot of valuable points and useful lessons that are highly relevant to households in which she makes more. In an article (posted within an article by Lisa Belkin) on the popular blog *Motherlode* for the *New York Times*, the Vachons write:

> Equally shared parenting can sometimes be confused with a 50/50 split of every chore, or with tedious and unloving scorekeeping between partners. If a couple finds a way to share doing the dishes, for example, one could then imagine them comparing (secretly or not so secretly) exactly how many spoons each has washed, and dividing every other household task as well. . . .
>   . . . If you peeked into the home of any couple who considers themselves to be equal partners, you would find no tally sheet. No list of tasks with names and check marks beside each. You'd witness no counting of socks washed, minutes spent mowing the lawn, or hours of

childcare attributed per week to each parent. No forcing each parent to do half the cooking and wrap half the birthday gifts. Instead, you'd find a parenting pair who has simply taken gender out of the way they work together—creating practical strategies to fairly share the load and the joys. They are both equally involved in caring for their home (overall), their kids (overall), and their careers (overall), and spend about the same amount of time doing so.

I wholeheartedly agree with the underlying message here about sharing responsibilities in a practical, logical, gender-neutral manner. You can't drive each other nuts in a one-for-me, one-for-you fashion. To reiterate, it's chiefly about creating a system to automate the sharing based on purely functional factors: who is better at doing X, who wants to cover Y, what's the ideal way to get Z done without conflict? And there's no "pesky scorekeeping." In the Vachons' words: "Paying attention to how much one's partner is doing (or not doing) is a toxic trap that is possible for any couple—regardless of whether they desire an even split of chores or some other ratio. We dare say it is most likely when couples don't talk about their expectations for handling all the work of running a household, when they don't agree on the core values of their relationship, or when they cannot come together as a team to figure out how to make their joint plan actually work."

The solutions that the Vachons offer are practical and applicable to every type of couple, with or without money issues. There is no magic formula to follow, just some words of wisdom to bear in mind. They stress that rather than focusing squarely on chore dividing, it's far more important and constructive to let go of obsolete gender roles and merely focus on forging a new way together. And regardless of income disparity, an equal partnership and a balanced life for both partners requires that we do the following:

- ◆ Prioritize problem solving as a team when it comes to tackling household chores.
- ◆ Be mindful of traditional roles that simply don't work for either of you, such as the expectations that you'll cook more because you're the woman and that he'll tend to the yard work because he's the man. Modify as you and your partner see fit in your family and lifestyle.
- ◆ Don't keep grim track of your partner's household contributions.
- ◆ Establish a trust between you and your man that you're both committed to dealing with the tasks and finding a way to enjoy doing so by modifying how you each approach them to get them done.

The Vachons also teach that it's key to remember that equal chore sharing isn't about forcing men to do more around the house. The results you get as a team benefit everyone in the household. "Fairly sharing the chores becomes a result of this mentality rather than a goal unto itself." Amen to that.

Beware of Burnout. Donna, fifty-three, makes more than her husband of twenty-nine years and wishes it were the other way around. She says this not so much from a psychological point of view but more from a burned-out point of view, wishing she could retire sooner. Being the main breadwinner makes her and her husband's lives harder. "There are many things that I do around the house that I prefer to continue handling—you might say I'm a bit of a perfectionist in certain areas. Lack of time makes it difficult for me to get everything done that I need to get done. I'm not saying that he doesn't do a lot around here (he handles most of the household chores). That still leaves an awful lot for me to juggle." My advice: she should relinquish more control and the need for things to be perfect to save her sanity. She might also save her husband's sanity by outsourcing some of what needs to get done.

Six More Tips for Sharing the Load

As Kathleen Gerson points out in her book *The Unfinished Revolution*, a 2007 survey conducted by Pew Research Center found that sharing household chores now ranks third in importance on a list of items generally associated with successful marriages (with 62 percent saying sharing housework is very important to marital success, compared to 47 percent fifteen years ago), well ahead of adequate income (53 percent) and even having children (41 percent). Marital happiness is indeed much higher when both partners believe chores are divided as fairly as possible or that they are working as a team, even if it's not fifty-fifty.

So how do we find that sweet spot where things get done "equitably"? Let's turn now to my six additional tips to taking the drudgery (and hopefully conflict) out of household responsibilities.

◆ **Pick your battles carefully and let your money buy happiness wherever possible (do the math!).** Decide what to outsource and what to delegate. Some tasks, like yard work or doing the laundry, are easy to outsource, whereas doing the dishes after dinner is not. Don't avoid hiring help for the sake of saving money if you really can afford it. Outsource as many household tasks as possible to buy time and bring more peace and happiness to your lives. Even if your partner says he'll cover certain chores, it may be more stress relieving to both of you if you hire professionals to clean your home, wash your clothes, or even grocery shop. After all, just because he says he doesn't mind doing it doesn't mean he wants to (or is good at it).

Case in point: Up until recently, my husband and I disagreed on how the laundry should get done. The way I look at it, paying someone else to do it is worth every penny because it saves me time. I pay $1 per pound of laundry—usually $35—and it gets washed, folded, and delivered by the next morning. My husband says he doesn't mind doing the laundry himself. It costs $4.50 per load, with usually three or four loads, to wash and dry. In total, close to $18 to do the laundry himself, plus the added time of changing loads and folding (a dreaded task that can take hours). We settled this issue once and for all when I asked him: what's your time worth? You save about $20 by doing laundry yourself, but it takes you at least three hours to get it done. Is your time worth $5 an hour? Is there anything more valuable you can imagine doing during those three hours? Even sleeping, in my opinion, is far more valuable. Outsourcing our laundry is now a way for us to better enjoy our Sunday afternoons.

How Much Is Your Time Worth? Do the math: take your salary, cut off the last three zeros, and divide by two. For example, $100,000 becomes $100, divided by two is $50; that's your hourly rate. If it costs less to pay someone to do something for you per hour than $50, then it's well worth it. The elimination of stress? Priceless. Although the thought of paying someone else to do something you can do "for free" can be a hard sell, it shouldn't be. Let go of the tasks and responsibilities that take you away from profit-generating work.

◆ **Talk about how to share responsibilities.** Husbands should be accountable for important responsibilities around the house. Remember, as Alison Armstrong informs us, a lot of times what women need to ask men for is simply to be accountable. We women don't want help with our implied jobs. We want tasks X, Y, and Z to be *their* jobs. Period. We need them to take ownership of these duties and have them be theirs, not ours. This distinction really helps.

To this end, it helps to create a smarter chore chart. Don't get so hung up on the quest for equality that you make life harder than it has to be. When Kate and Bill were first married, she cooked elaborate, messy meals, and he would do the dishes, always leaving the kitchen sparkling. As he got more confident in the kitchen, he'd whip up a few dinners, and Kate, out of a sense of parity, would insist on doing the dishes on those evenings. Fair's fair, right? The only problem: Kate is a horrible dishwasher. She always forgets to wash the bottoms of the plates. She somehow covers the floor in a half inch of water. At some point, they realized adhering to this rigidly "fair" schedule wasn't practical or enjoyable. Now when Bill cooks, he also does the dishes and Kate uses that time to fold laundry or organize the day's mail—things she's good at that Bill detests. The point is that you need to renegotiate who is doing what in the household. It's never going to look totally equal, but you have to both feel competent and that you bring value to the partnership. I've met plenty of couples who keep a chore chart so they know who is responsible for what and when. A dinner chart, for example, can be an excellent way to map out a week's worth of dinners and assign who will be the main cook on a given night such that, overall, the dinner duty is shared. But warning: if you keep a chore chart, be sure it doesn't morph into a scorecard.

◆ **Stop complaining, start hiring, and automate your life.** Save time by shopping online and scheduling routine deliveries of basic items you need on a recurring basis. You know that you need new toiletries every month or two. Plan deliveries of household needs at sites like Amazon.com and Soap.com. Other favorite resources of mine for "mom-sourcing" include:

FOR HOUSEWORK:

TaskRabbit.com: List your needs and your price on the site and it'll connect you with a prequalified "TaskRabbit" in your neighborhood. Grocery shopping typically costs $35, housecleaning $60, and handy work $85.

DoMyStuff.com: Whether business or home related, post a task on this site, similar to how TaskRabbit works, and service providers can respond.

BidMyCleaning.com: From carpets to windows to general housecleaning, this site hooks individuals up with local service companies that bid for your business.

OneClickCleaners.com: Whether you need wash-and-fold, tailoring, or dry-cleaning services, this site can help with laundry needs. It offers free pickup and delivery and special pricing for new customers. It doesn't offer services in all fifty states yet, so check the website.

FancyHands.com: For a monthly fee ($25 to $65), you'll be able to make a certain number of requests in that time period. The basic plan gets you five tasks for $25 and tasks need to be phone or Web oriented. For example, buying gifts online, managing your calendar, ordering supplies, or booking trips.

Dogwalker.com: Get help finding a dog walker or pet care professional in your area for as little as $1 per week.

Peapod.com: Shop for groceries and household goods that will be delivered to your home. AmazonFresh (fresh

.amazon.com) is also experimenting with a service in some cities, delivering groceries in addition to its usual fare of goods.

FOR "WORK" WORK:

PeoplePerHour.com: Find and hire skilled freelancers to do your PowerPoints, spreadsheets, and copywriting.

Fiverr.com: Tasks start as low as $5. In my experience, the odder the task, the easier it'll be to find a freelancer to do it.

oDesk.com: Hire help for technical jobs like graphic design, coding, and copywriting, as well as administrative and marketing assistance.

Elance.com: Similar to oDesk.com, post your job for free and sit back and consider the offers (and bids).

Scribie.com (for transcriptions): I recently discovered this site, and it has already saved me hours and hours of transcription hell. The fee is roughly $1.50 per minute of audio recording.

There are also local services catering to this new economy of "buying yourself a wife," such as the San Francisco area business Rent-a-Spouse. Go online and do a search in your own hood to see what you can find. If you live in an urban area, chances are you've got a potential spouse-for-hire somewhere nearby.

For a current list of websites, visit www.whenshemakes more.com.

◆ **Anticipate the small stuff.** I have to admit that one of the biggest, and most common, frustrations Tim and I have plays out at dinnertime. I hate arriving home from a long day at work only to hear, "What do you want to eat?" Here's how I feel about it: I've made decisions all day. Home is where I want to relax, not where I want to be commander in chef. But in fairness, Tim simply hasn't considered my perspective. He just wants both of us to be happy and satisfied with what we eat. Hell, he probably wants me to be happiest of all. But when women who make more walk through the door and hear that, we instantly jump to this question: why can't he make just one dang decision?

I've come to realize—about dinner and managing the household in general—that anticipating the small stuff goes a long way toward escaping conflict. If we forget to do the dinner chore chart for the week, then to avoid the dinner question, for instance, all I have to do is take five minutes during my day to text or e-mail Tim. Simply sending a quick message—Thai or pizza?—during the afternoon can ensure that takeout is on its way when I step foot in the door, or that Tim has stopped by the grocery store on his way home and bought ingredients for a favorite meal so we can make dinner together. This is just one example of how we can manage our household with far less stress. Small steps that make our lives a little bit easier.

◆ **Value his time, just as you would yours.** I can't reiterate this enough: don't assume he should cook, clean, and housekeep just because he earns less. Work is work. Just because you make more doesn't mean his hours are worth less. Instead of constantly bickering or, God forbid, nagging him to do something you asked him to do hours or weeks ago, ask for help in a way that lets him know it's an opportunity for him to provide. Rather than criticize, show appreciation for his time and contribution.

◆ **Ask yourself, What would a gay couple do?** When in doubt about how to divvy up domestic chores, without simply paying someone else to take care of them, it helps to channel the efforts of gay couples. I've noticed that they often know how to get down to business without fights and without any gender assumptions. There seems to be, for the most part, far less emotion and a lot more rationale in the conversations gay couples hold than straight couples when it comes to household chores. They're able to cut through all the emotional b.s. and just get stuff done.

Liza Mundy, author of *The Richer Sex*, wrote about this phenomenon for *The Atlantic* in a 2013 article, aptly titled "The Gay Guide to Wedded Bliss," in which she cites new research showing that same-sex unions are happier than heterosexual marriages. A growing body of research on household division of labor appears to reveal that same-sex couples do it better in many ways. And she addresses the question: what can gay and lesbian couples teach straight ones about living in harmony? She writes: "Same-sex spouses, who cannot divide their labor based on preexisting gender norms, must approach marriage differently than their heterosexual peers. From sex to fighting, from child-rearing to chores, they must hammer out every last detail of domestic life without falling back on assumptions about who will do what. In this regard, they provide an example that can be enlightening to all couples."

I myself have met plenty of gay couples who reflect this reality, many of whom have big income disparities. Mary and Teresa, for example, seamlessly take care of chores together based on who wants to do what. Although they occasionally bicker over chores that neither one of them wants to tackle, they don't spend a lot of time and energy letting such daily nuisances get to them. "Whatever needs to be taken care of, we just do it," is their motto. "We'll take a time-out and back away from what we're fighting about, but usually come back together with more level heads." Even though Teresa makes about three times what Mary makes, they don't have many issues about money and finances. Once again, they approach everything from a practical perspective and avoid power struggles.

Not everything is rosy with gay couples, however. I should also point out that they still experience inequities that can rival those in heterosexual relationships. Studies have shown, for instance, that they can just as easily fall prey to giving more authority and decision-making power to the person who makes more. But gay couples are compelled to devote more effort to the task of making their lives work, for they can't fall back on traditional gender roles the way heterosexual couples can and often do. And I think this speaks volumes to what we breadwinning women should be doing: leaving our gender roles aside and just devoting more thinking time to figuring out how to divvy up our chores and let preferences, talents, and plain old practicality rule.

While I think we can all agree in general that as a society we need to change the image of the home from one that's purely a woman's domain to a "domestic sphere" that's managed mutually by both partners, I do want to emphasize that in relationships where she makes more, you have to tiptoe carefully if your man isn't living up to your expectations. I've talked to enough bread-winning women to know that a common source of resentment stems from needlessly spending on outsourcing domestic responsibilities because he's not living up to his end of the bargain. Look no further than Michelle's plight in chapter 1 to understand this. She made the mistake of outsourcing too much, to the point that her husband was seemingly only accountable to his Facebook page.

So be savvy with your outsourcing and avoid overspending. But do give yourself more room to spend money when it makes your life easier and, more importantly, your relationship more fulfilling.

RULE #6 RECAP

- Studies show that you're bound to do more housework if you're making more than your man. For this very reason, it's imperative that you find a way to lighten your load or you risk serious burnout.
- The challenge is to find a balance when it comes to sharing domestic duties without stirring up arguments and feelings of resentment. Knowing how to communicate well is essential here, so you can agree about what should be outsourced and what can be a responsibility the two of you share between you or you each do individually.
- It's perfectly fine if the division of labor isn't fifty-fifty. But there are other ways for your man to contribute that can help offset the imbalance on the home front, "provide" in other ways, and make outsourcing some of the domestic drudgery feasible. Perhaps he's not doing the laundry or keeping the shower hairball-free, but he's taking the kids to school on most mornings and reading to them in bed every night while you unwind.
- Pick your battles and don't confuse your parenting role with your dishpan hands. Equally shared parenting is erroneously confused with equally shared housework. Separate the two.
- When figuring out who should do what, do so in a practical, logical, commonsensical, gender-neutral manner. And do not keep a scorecard.

CHAPTER 7

Rule #7: Break the Glass Ceiling but Carry a Shield

Alicia tells herself that her life as a successful thirty-four-year-old financial reporter isn't all that bad. Newly married to Simon, a fifty-year-old playwright, she's making an excellent living, earning twice what her husband does. Since they don't have any dependents, they are living large as "DINKS" (dual-income, no kids). But when I asked her about how she felt emotionally as a breadwinner, she nearly broke down. Not only did she lament about the insane eleven-hour days she works, but she confessed that she's "tired and exhausted 90 percent of the time" and worries about her future in a "fickle" industry that entails tons of volatility and unpredictability. In her words: "You can get fired on a drop of a hat for no real reason. Because I make more, I feel pressure—to keep my job, to not lose my job. I worry that I'm going to run out of options. I get worried that everything is going to be dependent on me. And that makes me nervous . . . I put a lot of pressure on myself, in part because I desperately want my relationship with my husband to be equal."

I could see the stress in Alicia's facial expressions the more we chatted, her voice growing shakier the more she revealed. She feels "locked in" and compounding her concerns are hopes of starting a family soon. She feels freaked out by what that might mean in terms of work-life balance and whether they could even afford to have kids if she chooses to change careers. My heart started to race just listening to her concerns.

Some of the latest statistics are revealing: According to a poll conducted by the American Psychological Association, not only are we women reporting more stress than men over finances and the economy, but we're also experiencing more stress-related symptoms, such as headaches, fatigue, irritability, and depression. In fact, in all categories polled—money, the economy, job stability, housing costs, and health problems affecting their families— women reported feeling more stress than men. If we were to examine the stress felt by breadwinning women in particular, my guess is the numbers would show that we're tolerating—some of us just barely—a lot of extra stress and, as a result, risk factors for illness. We're getting cut deeply as we break through that glass ceiling. And if we don't find solutions (ahem: carry a shield), not only do we endanger our jobs and work-family balance, but we jeopardize our health. In my own study, I discovered that women who make more than their partners report *significantly* more pressure to advance in their careers than women who make less. A great many of these women also wish they could spend more time with their families, but, they confess, work often interferes.

Protecting how you make your income without killing yourself is equally as important as ensuring the success and survival of your relationships. Fran Hauser, president of Digital for Time Inc.'s Style and Entertainment Group, sums up her secret to continued success at work this way: be high performance but low maintenance. She routinely gives this advice to the hundreds of employees on her team, many of them women. Translation: excel in your work responsibilities but don't require extra special care, attention, favors, benefits, or help from your boss or company even though you're probably juggling more than your male counterparts. For example, just because you're the room mother for the year at your son's school doesn't mean that entitles you to an additional day to telecommute than what's currently offered to other employees. (And if you do want to ask for that, then couch it in terms of changing the company's overall policy—not making an exception just for you.)

As a breadwinning woman, it's important that you continue to be a sought-after person in your work despite the ongoing challenges that threaten your income and marketability by virtue of the fact that you're a woman (and perhaps a mother, too). After all, there's a reason why we don't say, "I don't know how *he* does it all." Unfortunately, the double standard still exists. Women in this scenario must manage a different set of expectations from their male peers, even when they fulfill equal roles and responsibilities at the same job.

Let me make one fact very clear: female breadwinners with families who rely on them are living in a high-stakes world as a result. They can't afford to be overlooked for a promotion or, worse, laid off. As one mother of three so eloquently put it in an article for *Slate* magazine: "I have to do the same house/child-care work, *and* if I lose my job, my whole family is fucked." It's imperative that a woman bringing home the bulk of the bacon stay competitive and continue to advance in the work world. Unlike some women who decide to transition to being a stay-at-home mother (and have the means to do so, however temporarily), many breadwinning wives don't have that option and must tread extra carefully as a result. When a woman's family relies on her income, the working world is a landscape like no other, featuring many pitfalls and hazard zones that just don't exist for men in similar positions. And we intuitively behave differently at work from how men do. You will rejoice, however, at the bottom line: the same attributes that make us more vulnerable in the workforce can also be harnessed to make us more valuable and promotable.

Put simply, if you're a woman making the majority of the family's income, you need to create your own "insurance policy" for work security. But how is this possible? What are the secrets to safeguarding your earning power? How do you cope with the added stress of demands that typically land on the woman, such as children and family emergencies? Let's cut right to the chase with a gallery of ideas, many of which will turn conventional wisdom on its head.

Embrace and Reconcile the Double Standard

I hate to call out the obvious, but because you're a woman, your capacity to make yourself available and accessible at work is really, really important. Even when a woman makes more than her husband, she's probably still making less than the man at work with the same job title.

And when it comes time to getting promoted, statistics show she will likely lose to that same guy.

One of my friends texted me one day in a huff, as she was up in arms over her "two-faced jerk" of a coworker. "If I said half the shit he does, I'd be canned by now." She's probably right. Men typically get away with a lot more than women in the workplace. We know it. And it's not fair. So do we just play their game? Of course not.

As women we have to live up to pressure to go above and beyond at work just to stay in the game. This is in addition to the stress you're bringing home every night and having to make life decisions about things like having children (and consequently being absent from the workforce for a period of time). This unfortunate double standard is here to stay. But it requires that we employ certain rules to navigate this terrain successfully and reconcile the double standard to some degree.

I think by now we can all agree that, as women, we need a certain psychological acumen to win at work and not be penalized for our gender—especially in a male-dominated, traditional office. Breaking the glass ceiling requires playing a serious game of chess. Men have been at this career thing for a lot longer, and thus their way of managing, communicating, and connecting is still well entrenched in the workplace. And while, like you, it enrages me to even think that we should adjust our behavior to traverse these gender issues at work, we can't afford not to in some ways. At work, it's survival of the fittest. Here's how to play the game with grace and dignity.

Live by the 90/10 Rule

It's imperative to learn how to compartmentalize your life like men do. Men are master strategists when it comes to drawing the line between work and home. Women tend to be weak in this department, letting personal matters from home intrude on their work in terms of mental space. It's much more common, for instance, for a woman to worry about family matters at work than for a man to spend lots of time thinking about nonwork, nonemergency matters while he's at the office. The 90/10 rule advocates that while engaged in your professional duties, you stay solely focused on work 90 percent of the time and reserve 10 percent for emergencies. Obviously, this rule is more about how you allocate your mental space while at work so you don't get needlessly distracted or stressed out about home-related stuff; I'm not suggesting that you work for 90 percent of the time and handle family-related matters the other 10. This conceptual rule is about setting certain boundaries and sticking to them. Of course this requires that you have contingencies in place, so I'll reiterate the need to plan. In the past, breadwinning men have relied on their housewives to handle emergencies; now that the game has changed, women must plan in different ways—especially if our partner isn't available to pick up the slack.

If you're wondering about how to juggle staying at the top of your game as a breadwinner and parent, take some advice from a friend of mine: plan like a single mom. Her point is that when you're career driven and making top dollar while married to a man who cares equally about his career (but might not make as much as you), you shouldn't assume your husband will be okay with slowing down his work once the kids arrive, if they haven't already entered your life. Clearly this should be a discussion you have prior to having children but I see far too many couples miscommunicating these expectations even once kids are in the picture. If you need to stay late for a meeting at work, don't expect that he will be able to leave his job early to pick up Junior at day care. Make plan B (having a babysitter) your plan A and if your husband can help, awesome (and hopefully, 90 percent of the time he can and will).

When I first heard this, I thought to myself: "Isn't this letting men off the hook?" But then my friend's husband set me straight and said that of course he does his best to accommodate her work demands and help with child care as much as possible. But he never wants to feel as if his job is less important just because she makes more. (He told me this just as he was about to take a three-week paternity leave, and he was very excited about it.)

Acting like a single mom is not about letting your husband bail on being a team player. It's about recognizing that his work is important and encouraging him to participate on his terms—not because you nag him or because you rationalize that his job is less important. It's sort of like reverse psychology.

Don't Ask for Permission

I like to call this the "speak up but shut up" rule. The "speak up" part means talk to other women in your company or field about expectations, targeting colleagues you admire or who have "been there, done that." This will help you understand the culture in which you work and then navigate accordingly. Every company is different. The "shut up" part refers to keeping mum about certain circumstances you'll likely encounter, such as needing to leave work early to pick up a sick child from school or ditching a morning meeting to address a family crisis. In these situations, you don't have to tell everyone at work what you're up to *so long as your work gets done*. It helps to stay under the radar as much as possible when you're pressed to momentarily avert your attention to family matters.

Talk Up Your Performance and Don't Play the Woman Card at Work

Toss your emotions out the window when trying to prove points. When Raina, twenty-six, a sales executive from Virginia, learned two male coworkers on her team had been offered raises over her, she promptly scheduled a meeting with her supervisor. She didn't get emotional or make idle threats to quit. "I didn't approach my manager whining about wanting what someone else got but instead went to him with the facts," she recalls. "I hit above my annual number before the end of the year and I was going above my role and acting as an assistant manager. He agreed and I received the raise." A whopping $5,000, in fact, and a promotion six months later.

As I briefly mentioned earlier, don't expect additional privileges just because you're a woman. Ask for flexibility in your schedule based on performance—not based on being a woman (or a mother, for that matter). This is obviously not to say you should *hide* that fact that you have a life outside the office, but if you want to start working from home on Fridays or adjusting your hours to be able to leave work earlier so you can have dinner with your family, open the discussion with the honest reason of "needing to create a better balance between work and family" but avoid getting too specific. No need to say, "I'm a single mom and have no support system," or "My son's preschool hours shifted and I have to pick him up at four p.m. instead of six p.m. every day." That's too much information that can make you appear vulnerable. You never want your higher-ups to think your home life is a logistical mess or that you're prioritizing the personal over the professional. The general concept of "work-life balance" is gender neutral and not a new concept in the workplace. Run with that and talk up your recent glowing performance review or plans to attack the next team goal and how working from home might provide you with more focus to execute faster. It also might help change your company's entire policies for the benefit of everyone—not just you.

Pay the Likability Penalty (or as Steve Harvey Says: Act Like a Lady, Think Like a Man)

Sorry to say it, but it seems that we women pay a likability penalty when we succeed—it's incredibly hard for a woman to be seen as both competent and likable. I know, not fair (though some research finds men also are less likable the further up the ladder they go). But this fact will remain true for some time to come. Get over it and just keep going.

Fortunately women have inherent qualities and personality traits that, according to one recent UK study, can work in our favor as we climb the corporate ladder. Researchers at the University of London discovered that being "bossy" or "acting like a man" when you're in fact a woman is no way to win in the boardroom. Instead, women would win more accolades at work by staying true to typical "feminine qualities" like sensitivity, psychological insight, and good communication. So while we should *think* like men and confidently strive for advancement and compete with our male counterparts, we shouldn't forget to act like ladies.

Seek Mentors and Blend In

Find people who will support your professional path and offer sage advice along the way that further minimizes the risk of losing a job or promotion. In the words of Hannah, the financial executive introduced in chapter 2, "You have to surround yourself at work with people who believe in you and stick by you as a primary breadwinner. There will be ups and downs in a career. Not everything goes perfectly all the time. Executives are very expendable. You have to keep that in the back of your mind—you could be back on the street tomorrow. If your boss can find someone better, he or she should."

Hannah is right. And she's right about the importance of blending in, too. In her words: "To be a senior woman in corporate America today, you have to be able to hang with the guys. You can't make it so obvious or difficult for them that you're a woman.

Join in the conversation. I dress like a woman every day but I work hard not to make the fact that I'm a woman a liability. You have to assimilate. And hopefully that's natural for you. Not setting myself apart has helped my career. I don't want men to be uncomfortable around me."

Such advice may come across as fueling the double standards that still thrive in our society, but it's also part of the trade-offs we need to make if we're going to break that glass ceiling and dodge any cuts or bruises as we revolutionize the new economic order.

Mind Your Mood

As women, we're emotional by design. The key is to manage our temperament and bring our romantic partners into the conversation before we suffer serious psychological consequences that undermine our well-being and interactions with others. Whether we're upset by something going on at work or frustrated by a personal challenge at home, it helps to keep those lines of communication open with our spouses. Otherwise, the psychological stress can further put us at risk for conflict that threatens not only our ability to be productive at work but also our relationships at home.

Remember Your Victory Laps

In one of my first jobs out of college, I quickly discovered the importance of being your own biggest advocate at work—especially if you're a woman. When men brag it's just men being men. But if women regularly talk up their accomplishments, forget it. After producing a killer exclusive story for my news station on how a major drugstore chain in New York was violating workers' rights—a story that became top news the day it aired—none of my supervisors seemed to notice or care enough to drop me a line and say, "Nice work." After complaining to my coworker about this, she, more senior than I, gave me some invaluable advice that I still practice to this day. She said, "Farnoosh, you need to run a victory lap when you do something you're proud of at work." Literally, she said I should walk around the newsroom and make eye contact with my news directors, executive producers, and higher-ups while my piece was airing so they would make the connection and be prompted to recognize my efforts. It worked. These days, I work from home so a victory lap would be seen by no one. Instead, I make sure to send out e-mails to colleagues and higher-ups after a great *Today* show hit, or airing a video that gets more than a million views, to congratulate all of us on the wonderful work and to express how proud I am to be a part of the team. It speaks from the heart and is strategic at the same time.

Don't Get Too Cozy with Coworkers

Enjoy happy hours together and holiday parties. Business dinners are more than appropriate, too. But when it gets too "cozy" is when you overshare or listen to others overshare about being unhappy at work, hating the boss, fighting with your husband, or feeling a lot of guilt about sending the kids to day care. And this tends to negatively affect women more than men because when we gossip we tend to be harsher—and that can make us seem, well, kind of nasty.

As Peggy Drexler, a celebrated expert on sex and gender and an assistant professor of psychology in psychiatry at Weill Medical College, Cornell University, wrote in *Psychology Today*, "differences in how men and women communicate would suggest that the impact of gossip is uneven. Studies show women use far more words during the day than men do. . . . For women, it tends to be personal: 'I can't believe how she interrupts people at meetings.' For men, gossip is more likely to be about status: 'Did you hear Ted bought a Mercedes?' The darkest side of gossip emerges when it becomes the weapon of choice for women at war—whether it's equal rivals fighting for a position, or a senior executive protecting her territory."

Ignore That Silly Voice in Your Head

You know that voice. It whispers groundless anxieties that make you feel you're not good enough or worthy enough. Men have no such voices. Case in point: Researchers from McKinsey & Company say that an internal report at Hewlett-Packard found that women apply for only jobs for which they feel 100 percent qualified. Men apply when they feel they can fulfill 60 percent of the job duties.

Specifically, you may hear that voice telling you to attribute your success to good ol' "luck" and "a lot of help from others," when it's also equally (if not more) true that you worked extremely hard and were smart to recognize key opportunities when you came across them. Don't let this voice give you a complex about your accomplishments or worth. Don't let it cower you at meetings or job interviews. Be proud. Like men.

Show Some Humor

If you can bring the funny, bring it. Humor can go a very long way in making an otherwise seemingly harsh stance at a meeting (when really, all you're doing is disagreeing) more digestible. Of course, moderation is key. Use this strategy only when it feels right and when you trust your audience will appreciate a little sarcasm or poking fun.

Be Straightforward with a Dose of Helpfulness

A TV producer friend asked me recently, "Farnoosh, how do I go about managing my assistant producer without coming across as a you-know-what?" Would men ask this question?

She'd recently become frustrated with her assistant's lack of organization. She'd missed some deadlines and failed to read a few important e-mails that required urgent follow-up. My advice: firmly start the conversation with, "Things have gotten very busy lately and I've noticed you've had a difficult time keeping up with my assignments. Let's talk about how we may be able to work better together and avoid any more missed deadlines. Organization and timely follow-up is essential to the workflow. What do you suggest?"

This gets the message across that you've recognized a problem with her work and that the assistant needs to shape up—but that you are also open to helping and listening to suggestions. It shows compassion and authority at the same time. You allow for dialogue, as opposed to an open-and-shut directive like "Please follow up on those e-mails!"

Agree More

Not to be confused with becoming a yes-woman, the point here is that even when you disagree with a teammate or manager, try to start the conversation with some territory where you do see eye to eye. Then share your opposing views. It softens the blow but still allows you to voice your opinion and be clearly heard.

For example, if your boss wants you to be in charge of hiring a new sales associate and insists this person must be an Ivy League graduate, you might want to disagree in the following manner: "I agree that we should hire a new associate to help us better manage the flow as you point out. A strong educational background is vital. Now, as someone who's recruited workers at a number of college job fairs, I've got to say there are so many impressive state school alumni just as talented and eager—if not more—as Ivy Leaguers. I think we should cast a wider net and make it our goal to find the best person, right?"

Don't Opt Out and Expect to Get Back In Easily

The "mommy wars" might never end, and in the last decade they have seemingly heated up again over the debate about when and for how long a woman should put her career on hold to stay at home with the kids. This is an incredibly tricky area to navigate, one rife with heated opinions but no single solution that will work for every woman. In the last ten years, several high-profile books and articles have been written about the cadre of elite women (career-driven, ambitious Ivy League types with thriving careers as doctors, lawyers, bankers, academics, and executives) who decided to escape the workforce entirely to become stay-at-home moms. Obviously, these women had the resources to do so, mostly thanks to husbands who could be the sole provider. The conversation started with Lisa Belkin's famous (or infamous) 2003 piece for the *New York Times Magazine* titled "The Opt-Out Revolution," and it came full circle in 2013 when Judith Warner wrote a follow-up piece (also published in the *New York Times Magazine*) with an eye-popping headline: "The Opt-Out Generation Wants Back In." Indeed, some of the women who went MIA in the boardroom a decade ago are now trying to get back in . . . and having a hard time.

Granted, every woman's personal circumstances are unique and even the books and articles that write about the opt-out phenomenon highlight the fact that the broader story is much more complex than any headline can capture. Many of the women who left the workforce ten years ago didn't intend to stay out forever. But they didn't know just how hard nudging their way back in would be, a feat more complicated for some than for others. Those who managed to keep their toe in the door to some degree found it much easier to return; the others, not so much. And this makes sense: when you're doing the kinds of things that keep you connected and networked in a particular industry, even if you're not actually "working," finding an open door when you're ready to make a reentry is just plain easier. People will not have forgotten you, and you will have had your pulse on the goings-on in your industry rather than having been a total absentee.

To many women who've followed Warner's recent reporting, the most striking story is the one about Sheilah O'Donnel, a forty-four-year-old woman who was once a top salesperson at Oracle, banking a half million dollars a year. Once she and her husband (who was also at Oracle) started a family, she reduced her work to three days a week. But even that didn't seem like enough, as the stresses of running a two-career household put too much strain on the marriage. There were nasty fights about chores and who would take care of the kids when the nanny was sick. Eventually push came to shove and O'Donnel walked away from her job, thinking it would save her marriage (and her sanity).

But it didn't. She ended up divorced and is now earning much less than before as she struggles to get her game on again in the workforce. She went from living in a mansionlike house by many standards to a small apartment with her two kids. Warner conveys the true lesson in O'Donnel's story when she writes: "After one emotional session with a friend, her 12-year-old daughter asked what all the fuss was about. O'Donnel told her: 'This is the perfect reason why you need to work. You don't have to make a million dollars. You don't have to have a wealthy lifestyle. You just always have to be able to at least earn enough so you can support yourself.'"

This makes for an important lesson for any woman thinking about leaving the workforce permanently or even temporarily.

Sheryl Sandberg spends an entire chapter in *Lean In* on her dictum "Don't leave before you leave," which I think is very relevant for female breadwinners. What Sandberg is referring to is the self-sabotaging mental games we play in our heads when contemplating children and deciding on how we'll continue to work and "do it all" when kids come into the picture. It's common for successful women to scale back their ambitions and efforts in the workforce long before they have children (or even meet Mr. Right to have them with!) because they fear they won't be able to handle being both a mother and a career woman. As soon as she engages in that thinking process, she's likely to stop seeking or accepting new opportunities, and her career will suffer.

Sandberg rightfully points out: "The problem is that even if she were to get pregnant immediately, she still has nine months before she has to care for an actual child. And since women usually start this mental preparation well before trying to conceive, several years often pass between the thought and conception, let alone birth. . . . By the time the baby arrives the woman is likely to be in a drastically different place in her career than she would have been had she not leaned back. Before, she was a top performer, on par with her peers in responsibility, opportunity, and pay. By not finding ways to stretch herself during the years heading up to mother-hood, she has fallen behind."

To that I'll add: And what happens when you've derailed your career (and income power) and also find yourself single again? You'll be stuck.

Nevertheless, no woman should ever be afraid to leave a job or the workforce in general . . . so long as she is realistic about the consequences and has a backup plan for if things don't work out as she expects. Unfortunately, there's no litmus test to determine when exiting is appropriate. Clearly, the ramifications for quitting when one is the primary earner are substantial, so the decisions must be made carefully. Some pointers to keep in mind:

You owe it to yourself to continue to work even if you plan on having kids. You don't know when your career will take off, and you can't know what it will be like to be at the top of your game profes-sionally until you're there. What's more, you won't have a balanced view of your options once you're pregnant and under the spell of all those hormones. The "mommy gene" is not as powerful as you might think, and if you focus on work for as long and hard as you can, you'll likely reach a place where suddenly you've got lots of options to better manage the role of being a working mother. You'll be able to call more of the shots, set more of your own rules, and have the best of both worlds (this is true if you're working for someone else or running your own business).

Work hard and invest in your career when your kids are young. Careers are often more flexible than full-time parenting. Put an-other way, being a stay-at-home mom is a rigid job that's rarely reversible without a great deal of effort. As I've already noted, it's harder to get back into the workforce after a long hiatus. Stay in the game as much as possible and even if you do opt out for a while, keep one foot in the door.

As many working mothers have told me, it's much easier for

kids to be cared for by others when they are young than when they are older and start to demand more from their mom and dad in terms of attention and help. If you need to work long hours and spend lots of money on child care, do so when the kids are young and won't feel your absence as directly. By the time the kids hit middle school and require more of you, by then you'll have put in enough time at work that it'll be easier for you to make your own schedule and accommodate your kids' needs.

Renegotiate your shared parenting if you're already saddled with huge job and parenting responsibilities. If you're a mother of one or more children who demand a lot of your time and attention, and you're bringing home the bacon but your man isn't taking on his fair share to keep your life sane, then it's time to have a meeting with your mate. Rather than start plotting your exit from work, it's time to rethink how you can better share parenting duties so you can continue to perform in your job. And get professional help if you can't agree on how to do this. It's critical for the sake of preserving your income and the well-being of your children.

Learn to be more patient. If your husband is very hands-on when it comes to child care—taking on more than traditional fathers—don't expect a June Cleaver level of multitasking. In December 2013, the *New York Times* reported on a new trend taking shape on Wall Street: moms who work on the Street who have stay-at-home husbands. According to census data, "[the] number of women in finance with stay-at-home spouses has climbed nearly tenfold since 1980." In the article, Brandee McHale, a managing director of Citigroup's charitable foundation, said her husband, a former marine, does not multitask, noting that for him, "Laundry is an activity." But she also appreciates that he will focus just as intently on tossing a football with their children.

A few women said that they resented the fact that their husbands did not cook or clean up, but that they had trouble telling them so, for fear that they would sound as if they were treating them like employees.

When Kristine Braden, also of Citigroup, was stationed in the Philippines, she knew that her husband was never going to devote himself to hosting parties for her clients or setting a perfect table, the way some wives of male bankers did. (The couple entertained at restaurants or at home together on weekends.) Few of the men are willing to take on corporate spouse duties, like attending or hosting Wall Street dinners with the alpha men who work at the banks.

Make It All Work but Don't Burn Out

Perhaps the goal isn't so much about having it all or doing it all, it's just about making it all work. From my conversations with couples who've managed to do just that, one pattern rings true: the men in the lives of these breadwinning women are borderline amazing. They rise to the occasion in every way, both at home and in their own career pursuits. But that doesn't mean these couples don't have their gripes and constant negotiations.

Take, for example, Amy and Conner of Indiana. Amy, thirty-nine, is en route to becoming CFO at her oil and gas company, where she makes $250,000 a year. Her husband, Conner, forty, is a stay-at-home dad and former firefighter. They have two daughters, aged nine and twelve, and have been together for about twenty-six years (they met in high school).

Amy and Conner decided five years ago to have a stay-at-home parent. Part of the decision was due to the fact that Conner found it difficult to keep securing a firefighter position with good benefits every time the family had to relocate for Amy's job, which obviously took priority due to her income. But it wasn't always like that. Early in their marriage, the plan was to follow Conner's career as a farm manager alongside her parents, who had invested in some land. Amy quit her job and decided to get her MBA while Conner worked on the family business, but it didn't pan out due to an economic slowdown in hog farming (their specialty). "We took a pause. I had my MBA by then and had started a new job with a promising career. Conner was looking for a new career path. . . . We made the decision then to follow my career." As Conner puts it, "Our approach was not about who would earn more, but what job needed to be done. How the chips fell was how it would turn out." Amy and Conner relocated several times as she climbed the ranks in her career as an accountant, and there was never any doubt that Amy would stay on track in her career.

She tells me: "For me it's a natural fit. I was valedictorian in high school, graduated with honors in college, I was number one in my MBA class. I've always been driven to succeed and so Conner really supports me and what I do with my career. I work for a $2 billion company and the door is finally open for me to step into the CFO job. My guess is it would be a 25 percent increase on base salary and 60 percent on bonus. I couldn't do this without Conner's support. We knew we were following my career. We made that conscious decision."

Conner does have moments when he misses work and feels unthanked for the "job no one else wants to do," but he relishes the thought that he's the reason behind his kids maturing into confident, smart individuals. I sense that their religion keeps their bond strong. They are both practicing Christians who came into the marriage with a "this is it" mentality. And as Amy explains, "There certainly is a risk with one person giving up their job. Today I don't think Conner could go be a firefighter; he has spent so much time away from the field that he'd have to retrain himself just to qualify by today's standards. He really has given up his career. For us making the commitment, we had to assess the relationship before making that decision." When I asked her for some advice she'd give other breadwinning women to avoid burnout, she stressed the significance of being very clear about priorities and what's important to you every step of the way. There have been times over the past several years when Conner has asked her if she wants him to go back to work. Her answer is always no, of course not. Unless it's something he wants to do.

For now, at least, Amy and Conner are making their lives work, and I don't sense any kind of resentment as I do in some other couples where the man takes over the traditional child care role. But it helps that Amy and Conner communicate well and respect each other's roles and responsibilities. There's no drama, there's no room for burnout on either end, and they work on their relationship every year by taking a kid-free vacation together ("an opportunity for us to get away from demands of life and focus on one another"). The biggest bone of contention in their relationship is, not surprisingly, the housework. Although Amy can't remember the last time she went to the grocery store, she will often spend the entire weekend doing laundry (Conner was fired from this chore after an unfortunate shrinking incident).

Perhaps the most interesting nugget of wisdom I learned from speaking with Amy is that she feels as if the expectations are even higher for her at work since she has a stay-at-home husband. "If your boss knows that your husband is home with the kids, the boss will expect you to commit to more than if you were a dual-income household." Whether this is actually true across the board is anyone's guess; it seems like a plausible statement to make. But the hidden reality is that having a stay-at-home parent doesn't necessarily make the life of the working parent any easier or less stressful than it is for someone whose spouse works outside the home as well. In other words, the burnout risk still applies when there's a stay-at-home parent, and it may even be more pronounced under such circumstances due to the expectations.

Meet Carol and Jake. They live in Minnesota and have been married for eleven years, together for fourteen. They have a three-year-old son with Down syndrome. Carol, forty-three, is a product manager for a large retailer and makes about $60,000 more than Jake, an account executive at a small advertising agency. (Jake confesses that his ego isn't hurt by her making more money but that it's bruised by him making less money *for himself.*) They've managed to thrive despite having a son with special needs and financially supporting Carol's widowed mom. The one thing that bothers Carol is what Judith Warner calls in her book *Perfect Madness* the "mental work of motherhood," which falls squarely on her. While she has set up part-time day care for their son, she seems to be the one to take on the brunt of the thinking and planning. "Where [the child care] tips the scale [toward me] is, truly, the social and financial stuff. Balancing the financial stuff and managing the social calendar. I manage our son's calendar and have to reorganize my work schedule to accommodate his schedule on a weekly basis. That's where it tips. I do all the doctor appointments. I am the one who plans the most."

When I asked Carol what is the one thing that keeps her up at night, she responded: "The obvious thing that's always in the forefront of my mind is losing my job. It's as simple as that. What—if—I—lose—my—job?" And she makes a good point about the fact that having stress about one's job and confidence in it are two separate things. You can worry about losing your job all the while feeling confident in it at the same time. Carol also raises the issue about finding balance between working (and continuing to build her career) and making enough time for family.

These are all important concerns to which there is no single surefire solution. Fears of failure and worries about not doing the work-life balance thing well are common emotions felt by virtually every woman (and man!). These distresses are simply magnified by being in the primary breadwinning position. Burnout rates among female workers are on the rise, and being the chief provider comes with enormous pressures that instill an extra level of angst that other women don't experience to the same degree. This is why it's key to find healthy outlets for stress and coping strategies for managing negative feelings, which are unavoidable.

A study conducted by the Center for Work-Life Policy (now called the Center for Talent Innovation) found that although men and women both feel stressed at work, women disproportionately feel stress related to their families' well-being. Why? Because they see a direct link between the time they spend at work and the negative effects on their families (e.g., more junk food, more time in front of the TV, less parental supervision), whereas men tend to blame external factors (e.g., "society," television violence, bad peer groups).

What does all this mean for us female heads of household? It means we have to be extra careful not to let our successes kill us (literally and figuratively). We need to be cognizant of the fact that being a high-achieving woman puts us squarely in the line of fire for stress and stress-related illnesses. Some advice:

Commit to one hour of me time every day. Not once a week—every day, or at least several days per week. That's one hour that's wholly yours to do what you wish: go to the gym, go for a brisk walk, read, sit in front of your favorite TV show or movie, or just have a glass of wine while catching up with a friend on the phone. You need to build this into your morning or evening routine and prioritize it, just as you would work deadlines, brushing your teeth, or your daughter's soccer practice.

Stay rested. Speaking of power naps, getting the right amount of sleep is imperative to your health and well-being. If you're getting six hours or less per night, you're what the National Sleep Foundation calls "sleep deprived" or "sleep restricted" and are more likely to suffer from poor performance, health risks, a weaker immune system, depression, and even premature death.

Pay someone to listen. I know some people pooh-pooh the benefits of therapy, but if you need help with your stress, why not take advantage of it and share your concerns, fears, and insecurities with someone who's trained to listen and offer unbiased advice? What do you have to lose? Even if you must pay for this out of pocket because your health insurance won't cover some or all of it, it could be worth it (see Rule #10 for more on this).

Tap into your slush fund. Your "mine" account will prove especially handy in times of emotional and mental stress or when you just need a pick-me-up. Don't be afraid or ashamed to use it; that's exactly what it's there for. Enjoy guilt-free spending on the little luxuries that can lift your spirits, be it a massage, a manicure, a yoga class, or whatever.

Don't underestimate the power of little personal breaks and self-indulgent habits that help you to unwind and reduce stress. If you reach a breaking point or, God forbid, have a nervous breakdown, it'll be too late to turn the train around.

RULE #7 RECAP

- Breadwinning women may be breaking the glass ceiling, but many of us are getting seriously cut on the way up as stresses between work and home life accumulate. We worry about keeping our jobs, preserving our income, and maintaining a happy life at home, too. It's a high-stakes life for sure.
- To relieve some of this stress but keep busting through

that glass ceiling, it's imperative that we learn to compartmentalize our lives more, drawing stricter lines between work and home, and not letting all the double standards that still exist in society get to us.

◆ At work, "think like a man but act like a lady," seek female mentors who've "been there, done that," and spare your boss the specifics of your work/life challenges when asking for more flexibility on the job.

◆ Don't expect to be treated any differently at work just because you're a woman (and possibly a mother, too). In fact, the expectations on you are likely higher by virtue of the fact that you're a breadwinner. If you want special treatment or certain benefits, ask for them based on your performances—not your personal situation.

◆ Think very carefully about opting out entirely for any period of time. And if you do choose to take a hiatus once a child arrives, plan exceptionally well long before leaving the workforce and be sure to keep your foot in the door somehow.

◆ Don't forget to take care of yourself. Avoid burnout.

CHAPTER 8

Rule #8: Plan Parenthood . . . from Conception to College and Beyond

"**O**nce you have kids, everything changes." My mother said this to me years ago, and since then plenty of other women have repeated it. It's so true, it's practically a cliché. And when you're the chief breadwinner, kids really shake things up in ways that can be downright harrowing if you're not prepared.

I'm not determined to always be the breadwinner. Our financial status quo will likely change sometime in the future; the primary breadwinning position is often a moving target throughout one's life. Tim and I were at different places in our respective careers when we started dating seriously. I was more established in my profession and well on the road to where I am now. Tim, on the other hand, was unhappy at his job and still trying to figure things out. At one point, I said to him, "How can we avoid you being miserable this time next year?" He had just turned thirty and worked in the software department of a big health care firm outside Philadelphia. Unfortunately, his experience mimicked the classic work-place comedy *Office Space*. It was stifling his ambitions to start his own company someday, for it wasn't helping him learn and grow.

After that frank conversation, Tim started to take some courses in New York City and go on interviews, and things started looking up. At one point during our marriage he took an apprenticeship, earning only a stipend. I remember talking with him about the opportunity. I said that since I was earning enough money, it was a good time for him to take advantage of our financial situation to advance his career. It was my way of investing in our relationship—something that would pay off in the future with more financial security. And it's a lesson I teach other women who might find themselves in a similar position. As breadwinners, matching up with men who aren't yet fully established in their careers or who want to make a career change is much more common than we think. In fact, you'll recall the "genderational gap" I mentioned in chapter 1: it can sometimes take men longer than women to make the same level of income or rise to the same place in their careers; so a thirty-year-old man will have attained less financially and be less successful than a thirty-year-old woman (assuming she didn't take any breaks). This partly explains why dating can be so darn hard for us financially independent women. It takes a real man to want a woman who is well matched to him but is more financially successful (and it takes a real woman to want that man!). Which is why I tell girls who dream of Mr. Successful or who think they are already with their soul mate, who isn't "there" yet in his career, that sometimes it pays to invest in our men and encourage them to take risks.

Of course, this isn't possible for all breadwinning women, especially those who are already shouldering the weight of rearing children and don't have the extra money or time to have the hubby go back to school or take an internship. But you never know: a window might open up in the future, allowing you to encourage your man to take a risk for the benefit of your family's future. Be on the lookout and take advantage of it when you can.

Which brings me to the bigger picture: *family*. How can a breadwinning woman make parenthood successful, much less possible? I've touched upon family issues and parenthood throughout the book already, but in this chapter we're going to address matters more completely.

The toughest universal question a working woman silently asks herself when contemplating children is "How will I do it all?" The quick answer to that is *Not all at once*. As I mentioned a few pages ago, it helps to think in terms of just making it all work rather than the classic "doing it all." While we can certainly have it all these days, we just can't *do* it all at the same time. That's sage advice for any woman whether she's bringing home the bulk of the bacon or not. But female main breadwinners have an added challenge because they often need to continue working soon after having children, since their newly expanded families rely heavily on their bigger paycheck. No doubt, being a mom who earns the family's keep is one of the most formidable paths on the planet to negotiate. Without the right planning and preparation, it can be emotionally and financially draining.

According to a 2011 survey by the Bureau of Labor Statistics, 68 percent of married mothers with children under the age of eighteen work, and about a third outearn their husbands. The number of stay-at-home fathers has nearly doubled since the 1980s; approximately 626,000 men are the primary caretaker of children under fifteen while the mother is at her job. That's an incredible number. Clearly the socioeconomics of parenting are changing, but the expectations of Mom and Dad as individual parents should be following suit.

Get Your Priorities Straight

While Alison Armstrong is famous today for her workshops primarily geared toward women who want to understand men, being an expert on relationships doesn't mean she hasn't had her own hard row with the man in her life. She's frank about her personal experience in navigating her family's path as she and her husband have moved through different phases in their relationship as the parents of three children. For starters, she never ("ever, ever") expected to make more than her husband, Greg. She never even expected to make as much money as he did. For a very long time they paid a babysitter more than what Alison even made. And it paid off.

Greg was a CPA and enjoyed a great career at a Fortune 500 company. But then Alison's business partner retired and she felt that growing her company was a top priority. This meant someone had to make the children a top priority, and together they decided it would be Greg. "Too often in families these days both parents make career their first priority, giving their careers everything they need . . . and nobody makes the children their first priority. I have a very strong belief that in a family, someone has to make the children their top priority or the children will not thrive. It doesn't matter who."

Alison then talked to Greg about his job, which required two to four hours a day in commuting time and sixty hours a week at his desk. Greg didn't put up a fight when Alison asked him to consider leaving his job, but the decision they made together as a couple did mean he'd leave millions of dollars on the table. At the time, their kids were fourteen, nine, and six. Both Alison and Greg looked at the shift as an opportunity. For Alison, it would let her focus on her business, which was only modestly successful at the time. And for Greg, it would allow him to be closer to the family (and recover from a job that was wearing him down). He'd take on consulting gigs and work mostly from home. The decision wasn't so much about money as it was about family. They figured out how they could get by with their eyes on the prize: quality time with the kids and freeing up Alison to fully pursue her dreams. It was a risk they were prepared to take for the sake of their family.

From Alison's perspective, Greg's willingness to change his career's trajectory was a priceless gift, and she saw him as the ultimate "provider" now that he was taking charge of the kids. This went on for eleven years, and then they were thrown into the next phase of their relationship unexpectedly when Greg decided to retire from traditional work as a consultant and search for his next act in life.

"That's when I started to resent [his retirement]," Alison says. Although Greg went back to school and earned two master's degrees, having an entire household in school while she kept the business (and income) going became too stressful. Greg had seemingly retired from a lot of household chores, too, which further added to the stress. And one fine day Alison just broke. She remembers the conversation well: "I basically said to him, 'You have to give more to this family than you are giving.'" Alison had been biting her tongue for so long, and wished she'd expressed her feelings sooner. Greg responded just as she wanted, telling her that was fine and asking her what she wanted him to do to make the biggest difference in her life. This was when she told him it wasn't about making money. It was just about making dinner!

Alison is a master communicator, but her own struggles highlight just how easy it is to hit a snag in your relationship when circumstances change. Her experience not only accentuates the importance of keeping those lines of communication open in your relationship about each other's goals and expectations, but it further calls attention to the power of having your priorities straight when making decisions about who will work, who will take care of the kids, and how certain things (like making dinner) will get done. I think her story also sends a message to female breadwinners about maintaining an ongoing dialogue through the different phases in one's relationship, which will inevitably evolve, especially as they relate to the disparate stages each person goes through. While we like to think that our partners are, for the most part, on a similar path as we are, in terms of life stages, sometimes that's not always the case. You will find yourself going through certain things in life at a different pace than your partner, and you will experience certain things that he may not. All the more reason to plan your life based on which stage you're in.

Plan in Stages

As noted earlier in the book, Michael Gurian is a huge fan of thinking in terms of life stages, and this piece of advice couldn't be more appropriate than when it comes to planning parenthood. Although becoming a parent is surely a major stage in life, it's bookended by other stages that play into how successful you will be as a parent. For example, before having kids or even a partner to have them with, just knowing that you want them can change how you save and spend money, how you date and seek a mate, and how you chart your career path and even choose a profession that can accommodate all of your wants in life.

"The dialogue has to be bifurcated: there's the 'before children' conversation and the 'after children' one," Gurian urges. He's also sensitive to the biological changes that occur in a woman when she has kids, which can influence whether or not a woman wants to return to work at all. But for some women, faced with wanting to become a stay-at-home parent but not having the financial means or flexibility to do so raises lots of complex questions—questions that our current corporate world isn't good about addressing.

Gurian is right about two separate dialogues—"before" and "after." He's also right about preparing for the what-ifs of giving birth. What if you suddenly want to scale your work way back and take on the primary caretaking role? What if you hope to return to work but prefer to take a longer maternity leave than the standard six weeks? These are questions you should ask yourself and then figure out a way to plan for those wishes.

One way to prepare is to do what I advised at the beginning of the chapter: invest in your mate early and often. If you are a high-powered woman earning more and married to a guy earning less, then do everything you can to help him get the education and/or skills before you have children, at which point he will hopefully be in a place to contribute more to the financial pot or even take over the breadwinning role if you want to scale back temporarily. And if you're in the dating world, thinking about finding the man to father your future children, then make sure your chosen one has the assets developed so that he can later become the bigger earner. Otherwise, as Gurian points out, you're going to carry all the guilt and all the anger. According to Gurian, it's pretty natural for a female breadwinning mom to look at her man who is earning less and feel at least some resentment toward the circumstances. After all, she can't be with her child or children as much, leading to guilt.

While that may definitely be true for many breadwinning women, I've interviewed enough couples who manage to keep the negative feelings at bay. They are model communicators, though, who plan their lives in stages. What works this month, this year, and this decade will not necessarily work the next. This is especially true once kids are in the picture, when you're planning around their life stages, too. How you work around an infant's needs, for example, is much different from adjusting your life to having a school-age child or teenager. And remember what we learned from Michelle in chapter 1: it's relatively much easier to have your kids taken care of by others when they are young and you're climbing the corporate ladder or investing in your career than it is to be MIA when they are in formal schooling. And it's harder to off-ramp for a long period of time and then try to get back into the working world after you've lost serious momentum. In fact, Sheryl Sandberg points out in her book, *Lean In*, that "women's average annual earnings decrease by 20 percent if they are out of the workforce for just one year . . . 30 percent after two to three years, which is the average amount of time professional women off-ramp from the workforce."

In addition to developing good communication skills with your beloved, it also helps to work out economic plans and design a program that paves the path you want to take. Be strategic every step of the way, whether you're planning a first pregnancy or opening the door again to a kid coming home after college without a job. Just as Emma Johnson of WealthySingleMommy.com advocates a ten-year marriage contract, aim for a two- to three-year family contract that lays out your individual needs and wishes for making this part of your life happen successfully. And if you cannot seem to agree on exactly what to do, then get some counseling. Having a financial adviser helps me and Tim square away the financial technicalities of our relationship so we can find common ground for our marriage goals in the next three to five years and beyond. This conversation of course includes our intent to start a family.

Make it a goal to be as realistic and detailed about your family plan as possible. Don't dismiss the little things, either. Heck, I've already asked Tim to be responsible for designing the baby nursery when we have a child (and to which he's already agreed with delight). As much as I want to be involved in the joyful minutiae of picking out bedding, bumpers, and baby monitors, knowing me, I know I'll use it as an excuse to neglect far too much else. The questions that your family plan should address include the following:

- How many kids do we want? *When* do we want them?
- How will we pay for their education (private vs. public schooling)?
- Who will be the primary caretaker?
- What outside help can we count on? Day care? Nanny? Family? Combination thereof?
- Whose career/income will take priority in the first few years?
- When might there be a shift in income disparity and how will that affect the family dynamics?
- Who will deal with doctors' appointments?
- Who will handle the unexpected emergencies, such as a sick child? (And yes, this can be the person who doesn't typically handle the regular doctor's appointments.)
- Who will manage the children's social calendar (and go to play dates, birthday parties, etc.)?
- Can you foresee changes in your career that will influence family life (e.g., promotion, need for more schooling or training, relocation)?
- How will we plan for our kids' financial futures?

You can create this plan even if you already have kids because there's bound to be enough to prepare for if they haven't become totally independent yet. You might not be discussing how many kids you want to have because you've had them. Now the conversation might be around sharing parental duties more fairly, dealing with a child who has special needs (or is otherwise demanding more of your time and energy given his or her age and school life), or figuring out how you'll help pay for a kid who's gotten into Harvard and wants to go.

I'm a firm believer in having a man who earns less contribute to a child's financial future, including that of an unborn child. This is especially true for women whose income can support the bulk of the total living expenses. If he can't help out paying for a lot of the day-to-day bills, then at least he can chip away at those future expenses that you'll incur with children. This can be done through savings accounts that are tagged for the kids, such as a Coverdell Education Savings Account or a 529 college fund.

What if you're already feeling buried by planning missteps, because you frankly haven't been planning in stages all along, and now you're trying to make up for bad or less-than-perfect decisions made in the past? Don't panic. There's plenty you can do going forward. Some ideas:

Identify and solve "the one thing." What's the one thing that would improve your child care situation—and moods—as soon as possible? If your parental duties are running you into the ground then you both need to stop dead in your tracks and pinpoint the biggest source of stress. (There may be more than one aspect of your life you'd like to change, but for the sake of taking baby steps and moving forward, identify and solve one major thing first.) For example, would you rather take your child out of day care and hire a full-time babysitter so you and your husband don't have to race to drop-off and pickup each day, allowing for more quality time in the morning with the kids and letting you confidently make those five p.m. staff meetings or even go to the gym after work?

If money's a concern, analyze your spending and reappropriate the money. Find ways to afford the extra expense. Maybe paying extra for full-time care means forgoing the annual kids-free vacation you and your husband take, or hosting the holidays at your house, rather than packing up and flying the whole family out west to be with your in-laws. This will involve trade-offs and you may have a hard time reconciling them, but in the long run they'll prove worth it because you get to spend better time with your kids, continue to work hard at work, and avoid burnout. Case in point: My hairdresser, a man, is married to an accountant. They live in Queens and have two children under the age of five. They hadn't really planned for the challenges of raising a family with two working parents. Following in the footsteps of families around them, they sent their kids to day care while Mom and Dad continued to maintain hectic work hours. The result: never spending any quality time together, scrambling each night to feed and bathe the kiddies, and Mom never finding time or energy to focus on getting back in shape and physical health after two back-to-back pregnancies. Who has time to go to the gym with a house full of children? Their solution: hire a live-in nanny who cooks and cleans (she gets Friday nights and Sundays off). This may sound like something only the 1 percent can and would afford, but my hairdresser explained it actually was a cost saver for them compared to day care. The nanny doesn't have to afford any living costs, so she's fine accepting a smaller income, he explained. Now dinner is ready when they both arrive home, Mom can hit the gym after work, and the couple can enjoy a Saturday night out with friends without excusing themselves at nine p.m. to release the babysitter.

Aim for more flexibility in both your jobs. One of you may have more leverage than the other in requesting for more flextime at work, but it's something both of you should discuss with your managers. And look closely at each of your respective companies' rule books. When Gina, a sales executive at a big pharmaceutical company in New Jersey, wanted to find a way to spend more time with her children after her second child was born, she looked into her company's "job share" program, which allows full-time working mothers to team up and split hours and duties fifty-fifty. The trade-off is that you earn 50 percent less. But you still maintain your health and retirement benefits. She and her husband, a software developer at the same firm, desperately wanted to have a parent be more involved day to day. Gina was making more, but not by much, and because her company gave her more leverage to take advantage of flexible leave, she went for it. She didn't want to opt out of the workforce entirely, so this job share program seemed agreeable.

Not all companies have such generous programs and if your corporate rule book shows no indication of flexible work hours, you or your husband ought to present a plan to your manager that strikes a balance between what you need (Fridays off or a later start time in the mornings) with what the company needs (no slacking and improved results). Finally, if neither of you can earn any flexibility, discuss which of you could realistically try to find a new job in the next three to six months that offers more balance. Start getting those resumes and LinkedIn profiles polished and circulating. You may need to find flexibility in your job by finding a better one.

Don't struggle alone. If you feel like you're losing your grip on the home front, tap into the wide community of working moms in your city or town and, at the least, join some online community boards. To keep sane and for inspiration, spend Saturday afternoons attending mommy and me groups in your neighborhood, where you can connect with like-minded women with similar struggles—and maybe even solutions, too, like how to better sleep train your baby so you and your husband can both finally get a real night's sleep or how to talk flextime with your boss without compromising your income or your job status.

Barter with family and friends. There are small tweaks you can make to your day-to-day child care responsibilities without needing to write a check. With bartering—or exchanging goods and services with others in your neighborhood—you can successfully provide your family with more structure and peace. For example: swapping babysitting duties with a neighboring couple with a stay-at-home mom or dad. Could they watch your six-year-old after school for a couple hours while you agree to have their kid over for a sleepover on a Friday or Saturday night every other week so they can enjoy a proper date night? Can a neighbor drive your kids to school in the morning (since she's going in the same direction with their kids anyway) in exchange for you doing her taxes every year (or some other service you can easily provide)?

Ten Tips for Planning Parenthood

There's no denying that having a breadwinning mom continue to kick ass in the workforce can have unintended consequences at home. By and large children do need a mommy to be available to them at a moment's notice, and she is dearly missed when a "substitute" is around, even if it's good ol' Dad. Parents Amy and Conner, whom we met in the last chapter, used to trade weeks leaving notes in their children's lunch boxes. During a parents' night at their kids' school, they noticed that their older daughter had kept all of her mother's notes in her desk, but none of the ones from her father. Apparently she cherished contact with Mom because she got less of it. Now, that may sound like a sad story, but there's nothing wrong with admitting that as working women there will be those times when we just can't be there for our kids in ways we'd like or that they expect. And that's okay so long as we're mentally prepared for it. Our kids can grow up to be thoughtful, productive, and loving adults just the same.

The fact that Conner is a full-time stay-at-home dad puts them in the minority among families today (the man also works in the majority of couples where the wife is the main breadwinner). When I asked Conner about what kind of advice he'd give other men contemplating the role of stay-at-home dad, he was quick to point out that it's not something that one can instantly warm up to. He in fact never thought about it until the financials made that possibility the best choice for his family. It took him years, however, to be fully comfortable in that position and to see in his children some of the benefits of making that decision. Today the family has cool, confident kids who possess great leadership qualities, thanks to Conner's close parenting. But he's candid about the drawbacks, namely, missing the camaraderie and challenges that came with being a firefighter, and the difficulties of forging new friendships as easily in the "mommy world." But now that the kids are a little older and involved with more activities and organized sports, it's become easier for him to find a rhythm in his role.

So when does it make sense for a parent to take over the child care duties full-time? It's a question I get a lot these days, but there's no single answer. The decision about when it's economically smart to have a stay-at-home parent, instead of hiring a nanny or paying for day care, should depend on two key ingredients: income power today and income potential tomorrow. If the person who decides to stay at home is in a job that will never generate enough income to sustain the entire family (let alone pay for child care), then that person would do well to take over the child care role temporarily.

Remember that word: *temporarily*. Kids grow up, so no one can be a stay-at-home parent forever. For this very reason, my advice on this issue should sound familiar by now: at the least, the stay-at-home parent should do *something* to stay active and somewhat involved in his or her industry if the plan is to return to it someday. By "staying active," I mean going to networking events, working on small freelance projects, taking an evening course, or brushing up on skills through free seminars and classes online.

Pay Now or Pay More Later. Sometimes it's okay to pay for day care or a nanny even when the numbers don't seem to make sense (i.e., it doesn't look financially savvy given your income and the high costs of outsourcing child care) and you're wondering if having a stay-at-home parent is the solution. If either you or your man can make a lot more money in the future by staying in the game, however, you're better off spending on child care now. Otherwise, what can happen is you'll lose out on advancing your career and wind up making much less money later but have way more expenses as your children get older.

And if you're going to have a Mr. Mom, then regardless of what you earn, your man should try to have some income no matter how modest. More stay-at-home moms are doing it, so why not men? I realize this won't be for every stay-at-home dad, but it's ideal. Just as I would hesitate to tell a working mom to "opt out" for any lengthy period of time, the same goes for men. Why is it "so cute" when a dad becomes a stay-at-home dad? It's not. Assuming he will want to go back to work someday, he will be severely challenged, to say the least! Society understands that women take time off and companies are somewhat adjusting to that and not viewing the two-year gap on your resume as a deal breaker. But for men? Regrettably, I imagine the standards are much higher.

Now let's turn to ten tips to making parenthood possible.

Think Through the Identity Crisis

It will happen to you if you become a mother: you will face an identity crisis as you vacillate among your many roles—mom, wife, working woman. And you will ask yourself, are you a professional or a mother and wife first?

But that's not a fair question (unless you enjoy torture). Don't entertain those thoughts that make you feel "less than" just because you choose not to be a full-time stay-at-home parent. These thoughts can result in unnecessary feelings of guilt, rancor, and despair. Over dinner one evening on one of her frequent business trips to New York City, Kelly, the IT manager we met in chapter 3, confessed to me that she feels like she "chose her career" while her other female friends from college who *were* career driven at one point "chose motherhood." As women, why do we do this to ourselves? Do working fathers ever say, "I chose my career?" As she said this to me, idly picking at her salade Niçoise, her eyes drooped and body language shifted from confidence to inadequacy.

"That's a baseless insecurity," I told her. "You didn't choose one thing over another. If anything you chose to be happy; and while it's hard not seeing your kids all the time, you, working, is fulfilling to you, and your kids can sense that."

Brace yourself for the reentry into work again, too, after taking maternity leave. You will be torn, so it's best to anticipate this and prepare for it. As Kelly admitted to me, "For someone who didn't really want children, I was so affected. I instantly got 'it' when they were born. 'It' is all those wonderful mommy hormones that came . . . I thought, 'I could totally walk away tomorrow and not do this anymore.'" But, of course, she couldn't. She earns twice her husband's income and her job provides the family with health and retirement benefits. It's also true that she loves her profession and admits she's better suited for the corporate world. "I give props to stay-at-home moms. It's an indefinable job. Honestly I think I do better as a corporate executive," she tells me. "That's easier for me."

Leverage the Options

Sadly, the United States is not among the 178 countries that guarantee paid maternity leave (neither is it among the fifty-four that guarantee paternity leave). Under federal law, employees can take twelve weeks of unpaid leave when a child is born. California and New Jersey are the only states that provide partially paid maternity and paternity leave. Only 13 percent of employers offer paid paternity leave, according to the benefits consulting firm Aon Hewitt. (This will hopefully change in the future as trailblazing companies set new standards. In 2013, Yahoo made headlines with its announcement that men would be offered a full eight weeks of paid parental leave, half of what the company offers new moms, and a generous policy by American standards.)

Sadder still is the fact that many men and women don't take all of their available time off due to fears of losing momentum at work as well as their "good, hard worker" reputation among colleagues and the boss. Neither do they want to create resentment in childless coworkers. This is especially true for men who refuse to take paternity leave for fear of it ruining their reputation at work or otherwise damaging their perceived manhood. Unfortunately, the stigma associated with men who put parenting on an equal footing with their jobs is still alive and strong. Recent studies show that active fathers suffer the same false perception that harms career prospects for many working mothers: being seen as distracted and less dedicated to their work. They can be viewed as wimpy or "henpecked by their wives." It doesn't help that most employers still assume that men prioritize work while women do all the child care, which isn't always the case. So in addition to the financial hardships that unpaid or partially paid paternity leave can bring, there are all these unspoken pressures to stay working and not be the guy who shows any less commitment.

Although we all know that the workplace isn't as family friendly as we'd like it to be, that doesn't mean we can't leverage our options available. Each parent in the work sphere likely has at least a few family-friendly policies to consider, as well as his or her own position or status, that can inform certain decisions. Logistically, for example, who is at a better advantage in their career or field to work from home part-time or even full-time temporarily, become an independent or freelance contractor, or both, in order to be more available to your children and their needs? Who has the better access to corporate-sponsored health care or other benefits? Who will survive better psychologically if he or she slows down the career track momentarily or opts to be a stay-at-home parent? The job isn't for everyone, no matter how romantic or "easy" it may sound to some.

But be mindful that you can have your plan set in what you think is stone, and then find the need to change it quickly. As one parent of two young kids said to me about parenting and juggling careers, "This is a learn-as-you-go process. Just when you think you can do this like you do paint-by-numbers, you discover that the real world doesn't work like that."

That basically sums up the experience of Brenda and James, a couple living in Brooklyn who have just had their first child. I managed to interview them before and after their daughter was born, documenting the shifts in their thinking and plans despite their best efforts to have everything mapped out. Brenda, thirty-one, is the primary breadwinner as an employee at a large non-profit. Her husband, James, thirty, is a freelance writer who volunteered to be a stay-at-home dad while continuing to freelance part-time. Before their daughter was born, this seemed like it would suit the family well, for Brenda admits that her "sense of self is really tied up into what [she does] professionally" and they rely on her income. James, on the other hand, doesn't see his work that way and as a couple they believed that having one stay-at-home parent and avoiding expensive child care would be ideal.

But living this reality once their daughter was born became much harder than they had anticipated. For starters, being the consistent sole income generator (with important benefits like family health insurance) creates much more stress on Brenda. She went so far as to use the word "paranoid" about losing her job. And even though she negotiated with her boss to have Wednesdays off to be with her daughter without a pay cut, she finds herself working long, punishing hours and barely getting time to spend with James as they tag-team child care responsibilities and getting work done.

Luckily, the couple doesn't have any debt or loans to pay off, but they are "ultra-unsophisticated when it comes to finances." They don't have a mortgage (because they can't afford a home yet), and they don't even have credit cards (because they don't want to amass debt by financing any assets this way). And they are not aggressive savers. Obviously this needs to change in the near future now that they have a child. They can't be as loosey-goosey about money if they want to create a safety net. But I think they would do well to splurge on outside child care for part of the week so they can not only take some of the pressure off themselves as parents but also free up mental space to do and enjoy their "real jobs" better. And while this may come with a hefty price tag given their current income, it will pay off in the long run as Brenda continues to advance in her career and James can further establish himself as a writer. At this point in their lives and careers, they shouldn't be trying to do everything themselves, or, as Brenda put it, being "pioneerish."

Brenda articulated her concerns perfectly when she stated: "As

I get more responsibilities at work, I have mixed feelings about it. Right now I'm in a position where I'm being challenged to really stretch and grow, and it's happening at the worst possible time in my life now that I have [a child]. What I really frankly need is a job where I can punch in, work hard, and then punch out. But right now, taking a lot of work home with me has been stressful. Very stressful. The timing hasn't been right between my promotion at work and giving birth."

Timing issues are often cited as a source of inner conflict with women and motherhood. But there's rarely a solution to that from what I've learned. You can plan parenthood to the best of your ability but still be unable to control the precise timing of it all (i.e., when you'll give birth and how that will coincide with work obligations). The lesson: do the best you can with what you've got when you've got it; leverage your options as they become available to you; and adjust your course along the journey.

Formulate Plan Bs

This one goes without saying. You need a plan in which you set the stage for changing your schedule in order to accommodate your children's needs during critical time periods (e.g., maternity leave, early years, teenage years when activities gets ramped up). You don't have to prepare for all of these stages at once, but know which stage you're in and what's coming on the horizon. Any number of things can be part of this plan, from saving more now to paying for those added expenses later to investing in your man— paying for him to go back to school or get the training he needs to earn more—while you're more bankable so you can have more total family income later when expenses are higher.

Elizabeth, thirty-six, plans to do just that for her husband, Len, thirty-nine, who isn't able to find work in his industry, construction, where they live in a small town in upstate New York. They are a great example of a middle-class couple who have to consider plan B: making a move in order for children to be a possibility. It's also a way that they, as a couple, can have more options in the future and more money. Elizabeth also wants to be in a position where she can be a stay-at-home mother when the time comes. She makes about $50,000 a year as a successful freelance writer while "severely unemployed" Len works at a bakery, earning minimum wage. They are plotting a move to Ohio where Len can find better work and they can reap the benefits of being closer to other family members. "I finally let go of something I had been resisting for years," she tells me, "which was to hang on to trying to make our financial lives work here in New York. . . . Once my husband has a job where he feels more like a financial equal, I think it will feel much more like we are partners in our relationship, as well."

Prepare for Inevitable Emergencies and Inconveniences

Even the best-laid family plans can be mucked up by an unanticipated event or illness. Just be willing to make minor adjustments as you go and don't get too hung up on the frustrations that accompany life in the fast lane. Accept that there will be sick children, cranky bosses, teachers exasperated at your kid's misbehavior, overdue deadlines, inconvenient school closures, late dinners, parent-teacher conferences during the workday, temper tantrums, forgotten pickups, missed recitals and school plays, piled-up laundry, cluttered homes, stained carpets and furniture, and various odds and ends that will never meet or be "perfect." Prepare to live a little less perfectly as you tote around tots, responding to their every (well, most every) need. Don't beat yourself up when things don't work out exactly as planned. As the old maxim goes, "Done is better than perfect."

Amy McCready is founder of PositiveParentingSolutions.com and author of *If I Have to Tell You One More Time . . . : The Revolutionary Program That Gets Your Kids to Listen Without Nagging, Reminding, or Yelling*. I asked her the million-dollar questions many working moms think about: How do we come to terms with not being perfect mothers? What will the kids forgive and forget? What events should take priority? She had this to say:

"I think the key to managing the natural guilt is to make sure you are doing the most important things well—and that's spending quality time with our kids. Busy working parents don't have a large quantity of time, and let's face it, much of the time we do have with kids is spent 'ordering, correcting, and directing' them through their daily routines or to-do lists. That leaves parents and kids feeling discouraged."

The solution to easing that guilt, according to McCready, is to give kids high-quality time daily—ten to fifteen minutes of what she calls "Mind, Body & Soul Time." Each kid gets one-on-one time with you for at least ten minutes. During this time and depending on the age of your child, you offer your undivided attention by engaging in an activity the child likes, such as reading stories, building LEGO creations, or listening to music on iTunes. "Mind, Body & Soul Time is kid-directed time in which you get into their world and do what they love to do," McCready says.

I've long heard from parenting experts that if you're giving your kids what they need emotionally on a daily basis, then they are much more forgiving when you disappoint them by, say, missing an after-school volleyball game or are late picking them up. Just ten minutes a day to show them your love and connect with them emotionally translates to huge mutual benefits. Not only will you feel less guilty, but they will actually show an improvement in their behavior.

I love the concept of mind, body, and soul time. In fact, I could see this idea applied to couples in general, affording them intimate, distraction-free space in which to enjoy one another.

Bring Kids into Some Adult Conversations

"Is your mom dead?" That's what one twelve-year-old girl asked Margeaux Wolberg in school one day, prompted by the fact that Margeaux's mother was never seen among the other moms volunteering in the classroom or helping out in the library. It was her dad who always showed up. Margeaux must have been used to the question by then, because she answered it by taking out her laptop, typing her mother's name in Google, and showing her classmate that her mother was far from dead. She was "famous," the vice president of technology business operations at PayPal.

When I read this amusing story in the *Financial Times* magazine last year chronicling "Silicon Dads," fathers in the Silicon Valley who take on a much larger role in the parenting world than usual so their wives can thrive professionally, I couldn't help but feel a deep sense of pride for all the women who are bucking tradition and charting a new path as they reengineer their personal lives around their high-powered professional ones. The headline said it all: "The Rise of Silicon Dad: More and more men are juggling start-ups and Skype conferences with nappies, sleepless nights and tantrums." The article features Kirsten Wolberg, forty-five, who misses lots of school-related events but harbors no guilt. She and her husband, Michael, a former pharmaceutical distributor turned stay-at-home dad, are totally happy with their choices and believe that they are giving their two daughters the best gift of all: a strong role model in their mother. And it was a decision that came long before the kids were even born, as the couple sat down and had a conversation about how they would divide household and child care duties. That was when Kirsten laid it all out for Michael, telling him that having a stay-at-home parent was important to her but that it couldn't be her. They both realized that being a traditional stay-at-home mother just wasn't attuned to Kirsten's personality. Spending the day running around with kids and changing diapers was something that suited Michael much more than Kirsten, and working in an office was more for her rather than him. So the couple figured out early on how they'd manage to coordinate their family life.

The Wolbergs are a model couple. Not only do I give them serious credit for candidly discussing their values and expectations prior to having children, but they get bonus points for obviously communicating well with their daughters today (otherwise, how else could Margeaux have handled that insulting question so suavely?). I think it's essential for parents to speak openly to their kids, not just about their family's chosen dynamics but also about money, where it's appropriate.

And my advice on this front couldn't be simpler: Basically, for younger kids (aged five to eight), it's important to teach by example. No need to talk about money in literal terms. As sociologist Kathleen Gerson asserts, the most important thing for kids to witness is that you have a healthy relationship with your work and your money. If they sense that you hate your job—whether it's in an office or in your home—it won't matter how much you're bringing in. They won't appreciate it.

Don't underestimate the power of your modeling, regardless of your income. Know that you are a huge financial role model to your children. In fact, when it comes to teaching the ABCs of money, moms rule, according to a 2011 survey by Creditcards

.com. Researchers interviewed just over a thousand young adults aged eighteen to twenty-four and found that about one in four said their moms were the biggest financial influence growing up. About 21 percent picked their dads.

Moms are on the frontlines when it comes to identifying teachable money moments. If you have to stay at work a little later than usual, miss a dance recital because of an important business trip, or have Dad fill in as chaperone on the next field trip, be honest and discuss your job and why it matters. This doesn't have to be the big "we need to have a talk" kind of conversation. Even toddlers can grasp simple concepts like "You need money to buy things and Mommy has a great opportunity to work to earn that money."

While you're at it, no need to get specific and talk income. Stay away from "Since I make twice as much as your father . . ." The important thing to get across to your children is that their mom's job is invaluable. It makes her really happy; and it supports the family in a major way to be able to afford the life and lifestyle they enjoy.

Be Willing to Compromise

It's a cliché statement, for sure, but nowhere does it ring truer than in relationships in which she makes more—for part or all of the duration of the relationship. In the same "Silicon Dad" article for the *Financial Times* mentioned above, journalist April Dembosky chronicles the life of the Donahoes. John Donahoe is the CEO of eBay and Eileen is U.S. ambassador to the United Nations Human Rights Council. To say they've broken a few rules is an understatement, but they've called the shots quite superbly throughout their marriage. Now in their fifties, they've been together since college and over the past thirty-odd years they have raised four children and made accommodations along the way to support each other's careers, balance each other's needs and ambitions, and ensure the health and well-being of their kids. At various times one was on the fast track while the other leaned back a little, or one sacrificed a choice job offer to work in the city where the other was in school. I love the words they use to describe their union: "partnership" and "mutual respect." Even though the division of responsibilities—both domestic and for the sake of one's career—hasn't always been fifty-fifty, they are quoted as saying, "It didn't get tactical. It was philosophical." They are, put simply, the definition of what it means for each individual to make certain compromises along the way.

Dembosky's reporting mentions some of the astonishing facts about today's family environment. As noted in chapter 1, young women now top young men in valuing a high-paying career. A remarkable 47 percent of men between the ages of eighteen and thirty-four say that being a good parent is one of the most important things in their lives, up from 39 percent in 1997. And now fathers are feeling the stress of juggling responsibilities, too. It's no longer just a woman's issue. Both sexes complain in equal shares of feeling rushed all the time, and fathers in particular feel like they're not spending enough time with the kids. Dembosky brings up an excellent point: a lot of the shifting parenting arrangements are being spearheaded by the private sector in progressive places like Silicon Valley where norms are constantly changing to accommodate the evolution of modern parenthood. She writes: "In the broader San Francisco Bay Area, where the gay rights and 1960s countercultural movements launched a history of contradicting social convention, there is a cultural permission for men to step outside traditional roles." She further quotes input from Jeremy Adam Smith, author of *The Daddy Shift*: "Masculine identity has fragmented so much in terms of what men can be, and that is intimately linked with how men interact with children. There's not one way to be a good dad anymore."

Indeed, there's not one way to be a good mommy anymore, either. We're free to write our own rules as we go along and pray that social, cultural, political, and corporate norms try to keep up. And my hope is that the new standards being established in forward-thinking places like Silicon Valley can spread to other parts of the country. (No joke: at Facebook both men and women get four months' paid leave upon having a child, plus $4,000 cash to spend on baby gear.)

Plan a Living Will, Buy Life Insurance, and Save for College

These are all essential and fundamental when kids are in the picture. Here's my brief two cents on each of these:

Living Will and Trust: Since wives are more likely to live longer than their husbands or partners, estate planning is critical to minimize the amount that our standard of living suffers later on once circumstances change our income, as can be the case with retirement, illness, and/or the death of a spouse. And since we do typically outlive our spouses, it's ultimately we who decide how to allocate our assets—if there's a living will and trust that includes instructions for allocating assets. By having such a document in place, you assure your family that you get the final say about your possessions, rather than a court or having much of your wealth going to taxes. Health care proxies are also important, as they spell out your health care wishes and appoint someone to take over for you should you become incapacitated and unable to make decisions for yourself.

Work with an estate planning attorney to help you establish a living trust and to write a health care proxy, and appoint a power of attorney. Remember, you can change the will at any time. It's a good idea to review it once a year to make sure it still reflects your wishes.

Life Insurance: Although I already advised having a life insurance policy in chapter 4, this is a must once you have kids or other dependents, as it can help to protect your family's future. But as it stands, some 43 percent of working women have no life insurance. How much do you need? More than you think. Currently, the average life insurance policy for women covers just $130,000, about one-third less than the average male life insurance policy. If you're a healthy thirty-year-old with a child and bring home $50,000 a year, aim for a $500,000 term policy, which shouldn't cost more than $25 per month.

Saving for College: The earlier you begin, the more you'll have come the first year of college, even if it's just $50 a month to start. There are a few options geared specifically for the college bound. The 529 "qualified tuition" plan is a popular place to start. It's a state-sponsored savings plan (every state has at least one kind) that works much like a 401(k) or an IRA, where your money is invested in mutual funds. It is free from federal taxes and many states offer state income tax deductions for all or part of the contributions made by the donor. Withdrawals must be used for school expenses, including tuition, room and board, textbooks, supplies, fees, and so on. You can buy a 529 plan either directly from your state or through a broker.

According to a 2013 survey by Fidelity Investments, typical American parents with kids under eighteen and who plan to cover nearly two-thirds of college costs will meet 34 percent of that savings goal through a 529 plan. Note: Make sure your rainy day/ emergency fund and retirement accounts are well filled before allocating money to college savings. The fact is, college lasts four years, while retirement can last thirty or more. And between attending an affordable school, winning scholarships and grants, and working part-time, your child should be able to help pay his or her way through school. The financial burden is not all yours. Do as much as you can, but don't compromise your other financial needs because of it.

Agree on Parenting Styles

Disagreements in this department can lead to divorce, believe it or not. When I asked a close girlfriend of mine what wrecked her seven-year marriage, she confessed that, more than anything, it was the sharp disconnect they had in parenting styles that really sealed their fate. How to discipline and care for their beautiful daughter was a constant source of arguments and friction. She took a very laissez-faire approach; he was the rigid disciplinarian. She didn't want strict boundaries set about bedtime and sleeping schedules; he did. She'd let her daughter drink chocolate milk on occasion; he didn't. These may seem like trivial disagreements, but they can accumulate and fester over time, ultimately eroding the relationship.

While it's fine for one parent to be the stricter of the two, it's never a good idea to have kids with someone whose ideas and values about parenting are the polar opposite. You won't always jibe with your spouse over parenting strategies but it helps to be a united front for the most part. And it goes without saying that learning how to compromise is key in this realm, too. Amy Chua described her trade-off amusingly well in her seminal book *Battle Hymn of the Tiger Mother*: if she let her husband raise the kids Jewish, she was allowed to be the disciplinarian. Bear in mind that study after study shows that the happiest kids are not necessarily the ones whose moms stay at home (or either parent, for that matter). The happy kids are the ones who see that Mom and Dad get along. Whether or not one or both work outside the home, happy parents make for happy children.

Avoid Micromanaging

Mommy doesn't always know best. *Slate*'s advice column, Dear Prudence (written by Emily Yoffe), often runs letters from working mothers who rely on their husbands for baby care—but feel like they can never really rest because their hubby's not diapering/burping/straining carrots the right way. Prudie, a working mother herself, frequently reminds mothers that babies are pretty durable and there's no "perfect" way to complete basic tasks. As long as a baby is healthy, dry, and well fed, he or she is being taken care of. And constantly micromanaging a father (especially one with equally good intentions) is a quick way to start fights, bruise his ego, sabotage his self-esteem, and make his experience feel less valued. Be prepared to sacrifice your ideal method for relationship harmony.

Help Him Cope with Life Balance Issues

Now that men are feeling the same conflict and the same desire as women to achieve a happy balance in their lives between work and home, they need more help than ever. After all, they haven't been dealing with this juggling act for as long as we have. Like us, they want to be a meaningful part of their children's lives and be there for milestones. Psychologists and parenting experts have two big pieces of advice. First, ensure that Dad is keeping up to date with the family's social calendar and the kids' schedules so he's not left out of the loop. Plenty of apps can help you do this (e.g., Google Calendar, Deadline), or you can do it the old-fashioned way with a chalkboard or marked-up calendar in the kitchen for everyone to see. Tim and I share a Google calendar, which we can access on our phones, and invite each other to shared events like dinner out with friends and family birthday parties.

Second, and this should sound familiar by now, keep that dialogue open and fluid between you and your hubby. Let him know when he's done a job well, and ask for what you need from him. Remind him (as well as yourself) to stay as fully present as possible when spending quality time with the kids. It pains me sometimes to watch parents texting or talking on their cell phones when they're supposed to be engaged at, say, the local park or playground. All of us are time starved and trying to pack a lot into our days. But kids need their time with Mom and Dad to feel safe, loved, and protected.

THE COST OF FERTILITY

Attention, single women thirty-five and older: If you're already of "advanced maternal age" (ahem: thirty-five plus) and still haven't met Mr. Right but are thinking about children, it's probably time to consider freezing your eggs. You need to account for the reality that having your own biological children after this age becomes harder. And if you plan to consider going it alone by forty with a sperm donor, factor that into your financials. This isn't cheap, and you'll need lots of support from family, friends, and employers.

It's a Privilege, Not a Disadvantage

Just when you thought you had your family life figured out (at least for now) someone says something outrageously insulting about your chosen lifestyle. Though it can be great for everyone when dads fulfill roles previously dominated by moms, there are still some outdated masculine "ideals" for him, too.

In a *Bloomberg Businessweek* article from early 2012, journalist Carol Hymowitz profiled the new trend and discussed the stigmas that still exist. "At-home dads are sometimes perceived as freeloaders, even if they've lost jobs," Hymowitz notes. "Or they're considered frivolous kept men—gentlemen who golf." The dads I've interviewed have admitted they come up against the same perceptions. Stay-at-home dad Ryan (whom we met back in chapter 5) explained what he encounters most often after leaving his job to take care of his kids full-time. "Guys say to me, 'I'd like to be in your shoes getting to play house.' They don't understand when I try to explain that staying at home is more work than what work was. It's upsetting."

Undoubtedly a man's sense of traditional masculinity might feel muddled or even lost when he is elbow deep in diapers and friends with all the playground moms. But you'll be there to help support him and cater to his emotional needs so he feels appreciated. Remember, if he knows that he's being successful as a provider, even if that entails taking over some typical mommy responsibilities, he can squash uncomfortable feelings that compete with his sense of masculinity. And the good news is that today, a woman and her husband have a variety of options, and the world is wide open for whichever way they choose to parent—and live their lives in general. Remember, there's no one way to go about it. You have to find what works for you and your family.

And this remains true for all you single moms out there going it alone. You win the award for having the most strength and courage to do what you do every day without those extra hands. Jill is one such hero I had the privilege to interview. Banking twice as much as her baby girl's father (they are together but not married), she's on call twenty-four/seven for her child while bringing home the bacon as a television producer. She's wise beyond her thirty-three years. Jill summed up so much for me when she said: "My advice for women who make more than their partners? Run your own race, and don't be so concerned about making more than your partner. Focus on the partnership. He's gonna bring so much more to the table that may not be financial and that could be beneficial to you."

So true.

RULE #8 RECAP

- Breadwinning women who want to factor kids into their lives must take extra precautions, for a lot is riding on these women and motherhood cannot be outsourced.
- It helps to think in terms of "making it all work" rather than the stereotypical "having it all" and "doing it all."
- Plan for the stages of life and especially the many stages in the life of parenting children. This will make life—and parenthood—all the more easy. Be very open and honest with your partner about needs, wants, and expectations, and use the ten tips outlined in this chapter. Be prepared for your plan to be active and fluid in the sense that you'll need to make modifications to it as you go along, sometimes unexpectedly and drastically. Much in the way parenthood is a "learn as you go" experience, so is planning for it.
- Don't persuade yourself into thinking that formal child care or hiring a nanny is a bad idea when your kids are

young and you can barely afford it. These are usually the years when you're still establishing yourself careerwise and have a lot to lose if you totally off-ramp. It's more important that you have more time to be there for kids once they are older and demanding more of your attention and advice than when they are babies and toddlers.

CHAPTER 9

Rule #9: Grow a Thicker Skin

The idea of a woman making more than her man can make for a fiery conversation at a dinner party. I know it because I've refereed enough of those discussions in my own circles to know this topic can be explosive. It sparks a lot of deep-seated emotions from men and women alike. Suddenly everyone has an opinion. And the attitudes run the gamut from those who insist that no man wants to be with a woman who makes a dollar more than he does to people who think it's about time we blazed this trail. Question is, how can a woman who makes more deal with people who pass judgment and criticism or, worse, look down upon her (and potentially her man) as a result? A moneymaking girl's gotta do what a moneymaking girl's gotta do: learn to have compassion for the haters and come to respect them even if they don't play on the same field as you. (Or I suppose you could continue to hate them, but will that really get you anywhere?)

People who direct rude questions at you or attempt to disempower you through offensive remarks are often doing so out of a subconscious envy. Their issues are more about them than about you. It helps to keep this in mind the next time you find yourself speechless in an awkward social situation or when interrogated by someone offended by the fact that you make more. Over time, it gets easier to deal with all sorts of circumstances because you'll find patterns in the way people respond to you, as well as form habits in how to react to them.

While the mommy wars might be waning, sometimes it seems like a new war brews between women who earn more . . . and everyone else. And if you don't know how to traverse this territory safely, you'll be waging a war within your own relationship soon enough.

I've been to countless dinners where the check is automatically delivered to the man at the table. While we were on vacation in the Caribbean recently, a waitress handed me and Tim two menus: one with prices, the other sans. You can guess which one I received, right? When I asked her about it she replied, "Madame, you shouldn't have to worry about such things!" Obviously these attitudes are outdated. But how people view success—and view other people in general—affects how we behave and the day-to-day responsibilities we take on as women who make more. The right balance in my own situation is still a moving target. For example, I talk up Tim's career while offering few details about mine to certain old-fashioned people in our lives to whom I don't care to give clues about our income disparity. Tim and I also struggle with how vastly different our families are when it comes to money. Tim's side, like many families, seldom discusses money matters openly. If we display signs of excess or mention upcoming vacations to certain family members, I can feel the tension build up in the room, mostly coming from Tim himself, who suspects he's being judged. At my parents' house? If I buy anything—a house, a car, a sweater—my mom's oohs and aahs are often followed by "So, how much did you pay?" These are the two different extremes Tim and I come from. We're constantly working on finding our happy place.

One of the most interesting observations I've made while interviewing couples where the woman makes more is that some couples, in general, have learned to neither reveal nor conceal the fact that the woman is the primary breadwinner in the relationship. "To be honest, sometimes I'm embarrassed to admit to family and friends that I make more than he does," confessed my friend Jill, the television producer who earns twice the income of her live-in boyfriend and father to their two-year-old daughter. "I feel like it emasculates him." And as Monica, a senior executive and mom of two, disclosed in her interview, "We do sometimes get weird looks because we live in a very traditional area [where] women as the primary breadwinners are quite rare. People are constantly surprised when they find out, but we've never tried to hide it. We know some people might not approve, but we don't hang around with people who would make us feel uncomfortable with the arrangement."

Good for Monica, but the truth is that sometimes women who make more feel the need to mask the fact that they earn more than their husband. In fact, my own survey found that some breadwinning females feel that society disapproves of the income differences between them and their partner, and that they do fantasize about making less money so that their partner or spouse doesn't "feel bad."

There are many reasons for this, but ultimately it comes down to prescribed gender roles once again. The woman wants to protect her man's masculinity and the man wants to send a signal that he's adequately providing for his wife. In a 2010 *New York Times* article about "alpha-women" who outearn their male spouses, journalist Katrin Bennhold describes how one woman, an investment banker who makes more than five times her partner's salary, "keeps watch on their finances and pays for all big invisible expenses, like vacations. But in public, it is he who insists on pulling out his credit card to avoid, he said, looking like a 'gigolo.' "

Of course, while there's some humor in some of these "special arrangements," and women seem to be fine with pretending that the man makes more, to keep the peace, save face, or both, we risk disempowering ourselves if we constantly fake the economics of our relationship. A woman should never bow to pressure in a way that diminishes her contributions to the relationship or makes her feel *less* for earning *more*.

So how do you reconcile this challenge? How do you maintain a strong partnership at home while keeping the peace in public? Here are a few tips for walking the tightrope of disclosure, starting with the most essential one.

Grow a Thicker Skin

We all have people in our lives who try to pry, and it's totally acceptable (and advisable) to set boundaries, especially when you are protecting your relationship in the process. Anticipate nosy, inappropriate questions—and come up with a trusty response that ends the intrusive questioning. "Many people questioned if I was laid off or let go," says Daniel, who willingly quit his job to be a full-time dad. "The owners of my company even suspected that I was leaving to work for a competitor. People would ask, 'When are you going back to work?' When I explained that I was a full-time parent, many would reply, 'Oh, you're babysitting?' They don't understand when I try to explain that staying at home is more work than what work was." People like Daniel need to rethink the perspective. If this peeping person has no qualms about trying to dig into his personal life, he should have no problem (respectfully) firing back with: "I know it seems unconventional, but we've never been happier this way—and we don't expect everyone to understand." Whether you're the woman or the man fending off intrusive questions, it's easy to feel bullied in these situations. But we need to fight for our choices and avoid masking the truth. Who knows, maybe nosy Aunt Bess will be inspired by your "new normal" panache.

The couples who have to toughen up the most are those from cultures or families that are still living in the eighteenth century when it comes to gender roles. Ahmad and Farah, the Pakistani couple we met in chapter 3, are one such couple. Ahmad works from home and is the primary caretaker of their three children while his wife works long hours outside the home as a doctor. "It's been challenging for both of us to adjust in these roles," Ahmad admits. His mother visits from Pakistan for two- or three-month stretches, and while she's there, he tries to shrug off the undermining comments she tends to make. Ahmad laughed nervously when I asked what sorts of things his mom says. He replied that she comes from a different era and that without her help preparing meals, "we'd be eating Boston Market all the time." But then he also said that, while she's "not judgmental," she does slip the occasional "Oh, your wife isn't too much into parties," and "Oh, your baby needs a mother," implying that Farah is not like the traditional South Asian mother, wife, and social butterfly like the women "back home." He sticks up for Farah and the life they've created by explaining to his mother, "The culture here just isn't like it is back home. And when the weekends roll around, we want to be together as a family after such a busy week . . . and not have a number of social events on our calendar that pull us away from our children."

Patricia is a breadwinning woman from an old-fashioned Nepalese culture. She, too, faces judgment from her family: "Regardless of how much I'm making they definitely think I'm the one that should be devoting my time to cooking, cleaning, and domestic chores. My family still chides me for not knowing how to prepare meals and not doing this and doing that. I'm just going to hire housecleaners who come in once a week, and it's worth my time at this point to work on my business." I had to laugh out loud when she really showed her toughness: "If I show up to a family gathering and have grabbed some samosas from an Indian deli . . . they'll joke, 'Ha-ha, did you make this?' and I'll say, 'Ha-ha, I made the money that bought this!' "

The idea of growing a thicker skin also extends to the notion of dealing with social guilt and shame. Take Alicia and Simon, for example, the couple we met in chapter 7 who struggle with work-life balance and hope to start a family someday soon. She is candid about how she really feels about outearning not just her husband but her friends. As she expressed it to me: "I actually wind up feeling guilty that I make more money than my friends. I keep feeling like I have to treat everyone."

I totally get where Alicia is coming from, for I've had these same thoughts and feelings. It's why women like us can have a harder time holding on to our money as we give in to our inner nurturer and caretaker who yearns to save the world. But it's just not a smart way of living, for things can change on a dime in the future and suddenly leave us financially vulnerable. We need to learn to hold back from the urge to splurge on others all the time, as well as learn to deal with implied pressure to pay for others. And you know what I mean here. How many times have you been in a situation in which you're expected to pay? The check arrives and you're somehow the only one who notices it. Or it's the holidays and your siblings expect to receive extravagant gifts while they're off the hook in getting you anything. I say, stay strong and don't give in to that inner voice that wants to make you feel guilty or ashamed that you're not taking care of everyone else in the world.

Granted, sometimes the pressure to pay for others is just a warped perception in our heads. Alicia's friends actually don't make her feel guilty for making more or splitting restaurant bills, but she compares her relatively easy financial life to her friends who have kids and struggle to make ends meet, which leads to feelings of shame and guilt.

Understand, too, that it's not your job to change how others feel or what they expect. You can't, so don't even try. Just focus squarely on your own thoughts and expectations and follow through with what you know is best for you—and your sanity. This is why I say you can ignore the detractors on one level, but learn to love them on another level by appreciating where they are coming from. Hey, they might never be in your shoes or come to understand all that goes into being a breadwinning woman. And they may forever cling to old-fashioned ideas, obsolete cultural norms, and gender-based stereotypes for whatever reasons. You're not responsible for their way of thinking (or their happiness!).

Of course, it helps to have a reply ready to go at your next encounter. Here are some snoopy potential questions with which you may one day be affronted—and my suggested responses (some based on personal experience).

Why doesn't he go to grad school? "Good question. If that's something we decide is important to him and his career, then surely we will consider it."

What does he do at home all day with the kids? "What *doesn't* he do? He's so busy. Sometimes I feel super lazy compared to him."

Does it concern you that he's not as ambitious as you? "What do you mean by 'ambitious'?" (wait for awkward silence) "Oh. Career-wise? Not sure what you mean. I think we're both equally as ambitious and pursue what we love. It just happens that I make more."

Don't you ever foresee wanting to be a stay-at-home mom or taking time off work? You must! "Sure, anything's possible." Change subject.

Doesn't it worry you that your kids only see you for a few hours a day during the week? Don't you feel guilty? "No. My kids don't need me breathing down their necks all day. And we have more quality time together than we would if I were at their disposal all day, you know?"

Don't panic if you use versions of these responses to no avail. You will no doubt confront the same people in your life over and over again who will just never relent on their false, preconceived notions about "what's best." Gina, who just had a baby, faces criticism from everyone around her. She's got three strikes against her: she has a child out of wedlock, she's a woman who makes more, and her man is a stay-at-home daddy. Gina is well aware that people talk behind her back. Her biggest critic, though, is her own mother. Her mother expresses hostility toward Gina's chosen life, especially the fact that she makes more than her baby's father, Philip. I was somewhat stunned to hear that her mother would rather she be with a man who treats her horribly and makes a lot of money than be with someone who treats her well but doesn't have as much. When Gina told her mother that she was going back to work and that Philip would stay at home with the baby, her mother accused Philip of "using" her. To which Gina instantly responded, "How is he using me?" reminding her mother of all the hard work that goes into taking care of a child.

Gina is one tough momma. She knows in her heart what's best for her and her baby and is no slouch about expressing it: "At the end of the day, I know what kind of guy [Philip] is. I know what his potential is and it's nobody's business. If I wanted to take care of my whole family, if that makes me happy, who the hell are you? The dynamic is changing. Men can go out and find a much younger woman because she's easy to deal with. That's not our situation. I'm not with Philip because it's easy, so why should I face judgment because I'm supporting my family?"

I'll raise a glass to that.

Occasionally Let Him Pay in Public

I've mentioned this tip before but it bears repeating in the context of this chapter. Most everyone has a friend or family member with whom it's easier to just not fight. When Lynn and Jordan go out to eat with Lynn's parents, Jordan, who makes less, makes sure to pay, all to avoid raised brows. "My in-laws assumed that just because I earned less than Lynn, I was mooching off of her. They never said anything to us. But I could feel it." So, to avoid unwanted pressure, it's Jordan who pulls out their joint debit card and pays for dinners with Lynn's parents. "Even though it's our money and it doesn't matter who pays, it's important to me that her parents see that I'm an equal player in the relationship."

Obviously you don't need to play this dance every time you're in public. And I know what some of you are thinking: "Farnoosh, you're crazy." I know that for some of you this may seem absolutely ridiculous. *Who cares what others think? Screw them!* Well, there are "others" and then there are judgey folks like your in-laws, parents, close friends, and others whose opinions and concerns do find a way of interfering with your mood, mind-set, and marriage. When they're around, conscious subtleties like having your husband sign off on the check can defuse the tension. And that, in my book, is worth it.

Don't Overshare

Laurie Puhn, a couples therapist and author of *Fight Less, Love More*, is an advocate of being very clear about what you and your partner choose to share with others, including those closest to you. She suggests that you have a game plan already in place; talk with your partner about what details of your financial life you wish to remain private. There will be things you don't care to discuss with family or friends and other things that will be absolutely off-limits. But know the difference. It's important to know that both finding and adhering to that public and private line is key to building and maintaining trust and loyalty between you and your husband. Once again, this reiterates the importance of putting your relationship first. It might be difficult to face the critical eye of people who judge but ultimately it's your happiness and satisfaction—as well as your husband's—that matters. At the end of the day, if your mother is going to meddle no matter what, why give her more ammunition?

There will always be people who want to judge you for being different or who perceive something about your relationship that's simply not true. The key is to figure out what balance you want to strike between being discreet about your financial situation and being up-front.

For example, while the world now knows Tim and I have disparate incomes, it's nobody's business to know exactly how much more I earn or what our individual incomes amount to. For us, that's sacred information. And trust me, people have asked me how much I make or how much Tim makes and my response is fast and unapologetic: "That's not something we like to share," or, "That's actually private." Another version that I haven't used yet: "You're not allowed to ask those kinds of questions, sorry!"

Give a Little Bit

Couples who have been happily married for a long time will tell you that one of the secrets is to nurture the relationship in personal, routine ways. Tim and I like to sleep in on Sunday mornings and chat in bed. Busy working moms tell me that planned date nights are essential and that making a rule of not talking about work or even the kids while on the "date" is liberating and nourishing. It may sound silly, but try to roughly keep track of the amount of sex you're having from week to week, because a fall-off in that area can be a precursor to other problems in your relationship.

And, like I've said all along, respect the man. You may feel extra stress because it's your income paying the mortgage, but that doesn't mean he doesn't feel it, too. As women who make more know, guilt is a powerful emotion, and it can drive him just as much as it drives you. After all, you're footing the bill when he as a man is "supposed" to be providing for you. I'm sure he sometimes feels disappointed or frustrated he can't get you that designer bag, but he'll feel better when he fixes something that's been bothering you, like the disposal or busted kitchen cabinet. (As much as this may irk us modern women, sometimes old-fashioned gender roles come in handy.)

RULE #9 RECAP

- Criticism and unfair judgments are par for the course when you are a moneymaking woman banking more than your man. Love 'em or hate 'em, learn to manage the comments and "advice" doled out by others, especially the people who will always be in your life.
- Have a scripted response already in your head for the most common scenarios you'll likely encounter (see pages 211–12).

- Plan with your man what you are willing to share with nosy people and what you'll keep private. It helps to have a united front when faced with opposition and people who just don't understand or respect your chosen lifestyle.

- Understand that it's not just you who has to deal with unpleasant remarks and people who have no sense of boundaries. Your partner will be weathering this storm, too, so keep those lines of communication open and be mindful of his emotions. Find time to connect intimately with him routinely.

CHAPTER 10

Rule #10: Remember to Breathe

I began this book with a tornado of new facts and figures about where many women in developed nations find themselves today: earning a good income that can rival that of her romantic partner. And this, as I've described in detail, can have many unfortunate consequences. I've also acknowledged that women in general are living much better than ever before, and doing so by every measure, from health to education to access to opportunities previously granted to men only. We can take care of ourselves. We can make our own money, buy our own houses. We can earn as many degrees as we want, enter any industry, and pretty much take on any job (with a few exceptions, of course, like being an NFL player or a U.S. Marine Corps sniper). We can procreate without a mate if we so choose and raise our kids as single, independent mothers (and I think we can even supply a Y chromosome using some wild new technology, but I won't go there). But the goal of absolute happily ever after still eludes many of us. Most of us can't be fulfilled unless our relationships are thriving.

So how do we keep moving forward and push this revolution

to new heights? First we choose to live by our new set of rules and work just as hard every day in our relationships as we do in our careers. Although we tend to quantify our professional success in terms of dollar signs, titles, and reputation among colleagues, we must also begin to quantify our personal success in terms of how good we have it at home. Are you and your partner fulfilling each other's purpose? Is your sex life robust? Are you intimate? Is arriving home at night a joyful experience, not a total drag? Are the kids thriving? Do you talk over money or financial decisions without fighting? Are household chores done without anguish or arguments? Is there a lack of drama and negative feelings such as resentment? Are you, put simply, *happy*?

I realize that the word "happy" is quite loaded these days, and I also recognize that it's often a moving target. You can be happy one day but not the next. I use it, however, because it remains one of the most coveted goals we all hope to achieve on a regular basis despite the background noise of ongoing challenges and daily stress. And everyone understands happiness. You either have it or you don't.

And if there's one thing that we breadwinning women have working for us, it's our tenacity and industrious spirit. It takes hard work to get to where we are today. It also takes hard work to make relationships prosper (and to thrive when you're left holding the bag due to death, divorce, or some other circumstance). But I know you can do this. You must. And we as a collective force of female trailblazers must, as this final rule communicates, remember to breathe. It's how we'll keep breaking the glass ceiling. It's how we'll transcend gender stereotypes and social biases. And it's how we'll leave our legacies. After all, isn't that the whole point of doing what we're doing? Don't we want to pass on our resolve and integrity to the next generation of girls who dream of both the corner office (or some variation thereof) and Mr. Right?

You know the answer. I rest my case.

Get Help When You Need It

In the spirit of learning to breathe easier, it helps to remind ourselves of the real reward to this new dynamic that so many individuals—male and female—increasingly find themselves in: female breadwinners have empowered both men and women to pursue love. Fewer women than ever before have to marry because they face poverty, social isolation, or familial disgrace for being single; and very few men have to marry to increase their social standing. It amuses me that our culture calls the act of marrying someone who makes less "marrying down," as if that's such a bad thing. But the silver lining is that studies show that high-earning women actually do better in their careers when they marry men who aren't so high earning.

While some sociologists like to suggest that female breadwinners specifically seek out and choose lower-earning husbands, thinking that those men will be more available to provide child care, I don't buy it. I think high-earning women are just looking for love and if they happen to hook up with a partner who is perfect in every way but happens to make less money, so be it. And they will do what's necessary to make it all work. Besides, to say that marrying someone who earns less or is less educated is "marrying down" is just plain insulting and, frankly, sexist. Consider the double standard: In the *Mad Men* era, a career man with a college degree wasn't said to be "marrying down" when he proposed to a non-college-educated woman who earned her keep in the kitchen. So why would we call it marrying down today when the roles are reversed? We shouldn't.

Society might give mixed signals about whether today's role reversals reflect a positive or negative shift, but who cares? And while some women may feel responsible for their partners' feelings of inadequacy, I say, don't be. Use the rules in this book and their related tools to forge a new path for you and your romantic partner—one that ultimately affords you the opportunity to thrive in your relationship despite all the built-in pressures and social standards that still exist today.

Multiple times throughout the book I've emphasized the value of thinking in terms of just making it all work rather than having and doing it all, an impossible feat for anyone—man or woman. I encourage you also to get help when you need it, as this will help you to make it work, take things in stride, and breathe easily. I'm referring to the kind of professional help that you might need to get you through any rough patches or handle complicated financial matters. And for some of you, this could very well be the first rule to follow if you're the type who runs herself into the ground trying to take care of everything yourself. Nowhere does the issue of money and power rear its ugly head the most than when help is needed to sort through prickly disagreements, all of which can become exceptionally convoluted and complicated by the fact that you make more.

Don't assume you have all the answers. Even doctors need their own doctors and financial planners need their own accountants. And I am no exception. I might make a living doling out financial advice, but that doesn't mean I don't need someone else's financial wisdom to inform my own personal options and choices. I have a trusty circle of financial planning experts whom I rely on when I need help navigating certain situations in my life. Never underestimate the power of professional advice tailored to your own circumstances and risk factors. Reach out to experts when you cannot solve a problem on your own (*any* kind of problem, whether it's purely tactical, like setting up a college fund for your kids, or it's psychological, like explaining to your partner that it's not healthy for your relationship to follow some proposed course of action).

There's nothing wrong with a little couples therapy when you need to get past a serious barrier in your relationship (many of which relate in some way to money). A little psych counseling can help you both to be emotionally sensitive to each other and avoid further conflict to arrive at agreements more easily. It's true that money matters are largely to blame for breakups in relationships and divorce. So if you want to avoid this fate, you need to learn when to spot the signs of trouble on the horizon and have the courage to get help. This is especially true in a relationship where the woman makes more. It is a painful but motivating truth that it takes a bigger village to support and protect a breadwinning wife and her family than it does for a typical traditional household. While a husband may be capable of helping with some of the important responsibilities, for example, it may not be the healthiest move for the relationship. Know the difference between what's good for your finances versus what's good for your relationship.

Because You're Worth It

Life tends to throw us curveballs. We need to keep that in mind and allow for spontaneity. Although I've drilled in (over and over again) the importance of planning and strategizing, that doesn't negate the need to roll with the punches. And you will have lots of them.

Just because a woman earning more entails a unique dynamic that demands a lot of special attention and management doesn't mean she can't give herself permission to have fun—and still come out ahead. To this end, let me distill my six reasons for why being the primary breadwinner can potentially be good for your marriage.

You can be extra secure. Dual-income families are the norm today because surviving on a single stream of money is virtually impossible. As a woman earning a good living, regardless of what your husband makes, you can provide a cushion to get past the inevitable financial rough patches. And let's not forget that women in general need more money than men to get through life. Not only do we live on average five years longer than our counterparts, but we also pay more for everything from massages to mortgages, due partly to a gender bias in the retail world. Making—and saving—more money ensures more personal financial security day to day and in retirement. And all of this financial responsibility actually feels quite good. "For women, the sense of taking care of themselves—no matter what—is something to take pride in," says Kathleen Gerson. And, as many husbands have expressed to me: happy wife, happy life!

You can provide him—and your family—with opportunities. Your higher salary gives you the ability to invest in your husband's earnings potential. Think about it. With your financial help he could pursue a graduate degree, change careers, or start a business in pursuit of more income. It's the kind of investment that can pay off for everyone in the family, especially if kids are in the picture now or down the road. Should you want to off-ramp momentarily and be a stay-at-home mom, he'll be better able to provide for the family's needs in the interim. Or, if you need more money to support costs like day care or college savings, investing in your guy's earnings potential today can reap benefits in the future. For Christina, a former freelance editor who used to make more than her husband, investing in him meant selling her house, which she owned before the marriage, and relocating their family to a suburb of Los Angeles where he could find more work as a professional photographer and really establish himself. "I sacrificed a lot financially to support my husband's entrepreneurial endeavors," she says. "And there were some very stressful times when I didn't think we'd make it. Slowly but surely my 'investment' paid off and we're living the dream life now." As her husband grew his business and the demands on their family life increased with two young boys, Christina downshifted her career and switched to real estate while taking on the role of primary caretaker of their kids. Someday she might return to her previous industry, but for now, everything is working well.

You can count on more fathering. Knowing that their kids have quality time with their dad is something busy, top-earning moms tell me they greatly appreciate. Whether he's a stay-at-home father who manages the household day to day or he has the more flexible work schedule of the two, a father who makes less can often bring more to the table as an active and involved parent. And that, researchers say, is an important factor in a happy marriage. In fact, for both spouses, successful marriages partly hinge on the mother's perception of the father-child relationship, according to a recent joint study by Brigham Young University and Utah State University. Amy, the high-ranking business executive we met in chapter 7, has been happily married to Conner, a firefighter turned stay-at-home dad, for close to twenty years. She shares a day in their life: "While I was at work and commuting from eight a.m. to eight p.m., my husband fixed a couple of kitchen cabinets, a bedroom door that wouldn't close properly, and two leaky faucets. He cleaned up the mangled trampoline from a recent storm, went to the grocery store, took my daughter to the eye doctor, and then picked up dinner. And he never complains. When I told him about our interview, he said, 'Man or woman, someone has to be there and do what needs to be done with the kids and the house.' I am so lucky. . . . All I had to do on the home front tonight is hang out with him and my kids, the true definition of luxury."

You can lean further in. Some women admit to me that, while they would readily die for their children, they are way happier in a boardroom meeting than at a Tumblin' Tots session. And they don't feel guilty about it. They're proud of the fact that their salary, benefits and annual bonuses help to keep the lights on and then some at home. They also know that their happiness at work translates into a happy life for everyone. So if the boss opens the door for a promotion that may mean missing a few family dinners every month, breadwinning wives don't have to feel conflicted.

Your kids will appreciate you. Take heart in the observation Gerson makes about the results of a survey, as stated in her book: "Despite the popular fear that employed mothers deprive their children of essential maternal attention, no [adult] cited a mother's job as a cause of neglect. To the contrary, they were more likely to see working as an indication of a mother's love."

You can be role models . . . and leave a legacy. Along the journey as husband and wife, as you commit to crushing gender expectations and raising a family by your own mutually acceptable rules, you will also have the awesome responsibility of being role models for your children—especially your daughters—who will look to you for guidance and setting the example. Our girls must be convinced that they can look forward to being top-earning women, to achieve success, love, family, and happiness, no matter the digits on her paycheck. Just like Mom did.

Disengage from the Mommy War

Let me be clear that I don't intend any of my rules, lessons, or messages to fuel the mommy wars. Stay-at-home mothers may not provide a salary, but they do indeed provide. And many of them may very well find themselves in the breadwinning role one day. Be grateful for these stay-at-home parents, including the daddies, who help keep the trains running on time beyond the income-generating office setting. They are often the hidden engines behind our schools, charities, and the community at large. After all, we all strive for the same things in life: to be healthy, happy, and productive (there's that word again: happy). And none of us will get there without the help of others, regardless of how much we make or whether or not we have a "real job." We also all want to be of service to others—to know that what we do daily improves the lives of others. And again, this is true whether we generate an income or not.

As a woman who makes more, you will face opposition. You will feel threatened and get defensive on occasion. You will be judged. You will judge others when you least expect it or even when you know you shouldn't. And you will have times when you feel incredibly guilty and perhaps intimidated (by none other than the woman who hasn't worked outside the home in twenty-odd years because she's devoted her entire life to raising a family). Accept this reality and see if you can rise above it. In the inspiring words of Sheryl Sandberg: "The gender wars need an immediate and lasting peace. True equality will be achieved only when we *all* fight the stereotypes that hold us back. Feeling threatened by others' choices pulls us all down. Instead, we should funnel our energy into breaking this cycle."

Sandberg is absolutely right. She's also right in calling for an end to social norms that keep us feeling bad about ourselves and the roles we fill (or don't fill). This is especially true in the world of "when she makes more," for why should a breadwinning woman feel bad about her income power? Why does a young child whose mother is never at school feel awkward about it around friends? This needs to change. But I think we're already on the road there, and if you're reading this book then you're participating. Soon enough, we'll witness our work standards shift, too, as they become much less inflexible and unfair—helping the breadwinning woman to be all the more supported and empowered. Which will make the options we have as individuals, couples, and families that much easier to choose, without the guilt, shame, and personal conflict.

If there's anything that I want you to remember most from this book, it's that you're worth it. And your relationships are worth it, too. Women who do not hide their talents and gifts have a much stronger sense of worth and can parlay that into a powerful, enriching relationship with a partner. They can also share their success with children who aspire when they grow up to be equally successful, regardless of their gender. When we feel good about ourselves, we make healthier choices—financial and beyond—for ourselves and have a positive influence on those who depend on us to fulfill their own life's purpose. You need to own your accomplishments and be role models for the young men and women growing up so that they may become part of a similarly functioning family. In other words, pay it forward.

Let's Get This Party Started

My inspiration for writing this book can be summed up in a single thought process I had one evening with my notebook. *Here I've arrived at this place of financial empowerment, career success, finding the love of my life. I climbed the freaking mountain, shot for the stars, and earned it all on my own. But where's my champagne? Where's the party? Nobody's giving a toast.*

To the contrary, I felt a little bit like a failure, considering the amount of hostility in the world toward my breadwinning status.

But now it's time to get this party started once and for all. I'll be the first to raise my glass to all the hardworking women who bring home the bacon and the wonderful men who love them. Join me.

I hope it's obvious to you that this book isn't just a practical how-to for a specific group of women out there; it's also a conversation starter for millions of other women—young and old alike—who hope to be part of the change we all need in our society. I invite you to continue the discussion at www.facebook.com/when shemakesmore as well as on www.whenshemakesmore.com, where you can join me to talk about the issues, share new ideas, and support one another. There, you'll also be able to access resources and practical tools, as well as watch some of the women interviewed in this book, all to learn more about how to reach your goals and live your best life When You Make More.

Now, take a deep breath. And go forward.

ACKNOWLEDGMENTS

I may have had the idea to write this book, but that, alone, would have never been enough to bring it to life. It is thanks to a dream team of collaborators and supporters that *When She Makes More* is now a reality.

First, thank you to my literary agent and friend Bonnie Solow. There are few people in life who will believe in you unconditionally and be your advocate, even when you're ready to call it quits. For me, Bonnie is the epitome of that and a gem of a person. More than once in the initial stages I was prepared to abandon this project and its message. I had big doubts. But Bonnie never left my side. Her unrelenting commitment, leadership, and honest feedback became our guiding light. She gave my little idea its wings—the biggest it could have ever imagined.

I am also incredibly grateful for my writing partner, Kristin Loberg, whose brilliance, devotion, and grace are simply unmatched. The plight of the modern woman, her partner, and her paycheck is far from a simple subject to tackle. There was as much emotional terrain as there was technical to traverse. Kristin, much braver and wiser than I, tirelessly and valiantly steered us toward the promised land. She is an absolute gift and with tremendous thanks to her, this book discovered not only the perfect words, but its heart and soul. And I, in the process, found a dear friend.

Thank you to my esteemed editor, Caroline Sutton, and her sophisticated team at Hudson Street Press: Christina Rodriguez, Courtney Nobile, and Ashley Pattison McClay. You generously gave this book the most nurturing home. Thank you for your leadership, support, and so much patience!

I will be forever indebted to my brilliant brain trust that helped me strategize and share *When She Makes More* and its message with the world. This includes the most superb agent in the world, Adam Kirschner; my extraordinary publicity team at Krupp Kommunications led by the formidable Heidi Krupp; as well as my digital marketing maven, Selena Soo. I also owe a supersize thank-you to Ramit Sethi, Kavita Patel, Derek Halpern, and Nathalie Lussier for their invaluable feedback and encouragement. And for helping me put my best foot forward online, a big thank-you to Cheryl Binnie, as well as Adam Scher and Chris Langer of Operation: CMYK.

A special thank-you to Brad Klontz, who so generously and enthusiastically got on board with me from the very first day I imagined this book. You helped me turn my guesses into facts and made this book and its message so much stronger.

This project would not have been possible without the more than one thousand brave women nationwide who openly shared their attitudes and insights on this delicate subject. Many kindly handed over hours of their busy lives to be documented and help fellow women who make more reach their goals. You inspired me and now, you have inspired top-earning women everywhere to pursue their best life.

Special thanks to my dear friends Kate Dailey, Dustin Newcombe, and Meghan Stevenson. You took my message from good to great in those early days when I was eager for honest, patient listeners and gifted editors. You showed me a smarter way and helped me achieve my goals.

Finally, I am so thankful for my family, who has cheered me on every step of the way since I could walk and talk: my mom and dad, Adam and Sheila Torabi. Thank you for raising me to stand on my own two feet. Thank you to my amazing brother, Todd, who keeps me smiling, laughing, and learning. I would also like to thank Eileen and Phil Jaquith, as well as Doug, Jean, Bradley, Kate, and the entire Dussinger family for their love and support.

And to my dear husband, Tim, thank you mostly for your acceptance, your patience, unconditional love, and for forever being my biggest champion. I can't wait for our next chapter!

NOTES

Introduction

ix **The media have had a field day:** To get a sense of how popular the topic of "women on the rise" has become, just search Google on the term and further check out Catherine Rampell's article for the *New York Times*, "U.S. Women on the Rise as Family Breadwinner," May 29, 2013, http://www.nytimes.com/2013/05/30/business/economy/women -as-family-breadwinner-on-the-rise-study-says.html. Also see Belinda Luscombe's article for *Time* magazine, "Workplace Salaries: At Last, Women on Top," September 1, 2010, http://content.time.com/time/business/article/0,8599,2015274,00.html.

xi **place an emphasis on career aspirations:** Eileen Patten and Kim Parker, "A Gender Reversal on Career Aspirations," Pew Research Social & Demographic Trends, April 19, 2012, http://www.pewsocial trends.org/2012/04/19/a-gender-reversal-on-career-aspirations/.

xi **By the end of 2012:** Ibid.

xii **women under the age of thirty:** This figure comes from James Chung of Reach Advisors (http://reachadvisors.com/). He spent more than a year analyzing data from the Census Bureau's American Community Survey. See Belinda Luscombe, "Workplace Salaries: At Last, Women on Top," *Time*, September 1, 2010, http://content.time.com/time/busi ness/article/0,8599,2015274,00.html.

xii **Of all married couples:** Rampell, "U.S. Women on the Rise as Family Breadwinner."

xii **two distinct groups make up the majority of the breadwinning women:** Wendy Wang, Kim Parker, and Paul Taylor, "Breadwinner Moms," Pew Research Social & Demographic Trends, May 29, 2013, http://www.pewsocialtrends.org/2013/05/29/breadwinner-moms/.

xii **discuss their finances more than they do their sex life:** "Fewer Mass Affluent Americans Express Concerns about Retirement and Health Care Costs, According to Merrill Edge Report," Reuters, October 24, 2012, http://www.reuters.com/article/2012/10/24/idUS131876+24-Oct -2012+BW20121024.

xii **"generally better for a marriage if the husband earns more than his wife":** Hanna Rosin, "Farewell, Male Breadwinners," *Slate*, May 29, 2013, http://www.slate.com/blogs/xx_factor/2013/05/29/pew_study_ on_female_breadwinners_in_four_out_of_10_households_with_ kids.html. See the original study for Pew by Wang, Parker, and Taylor, "Breadwinner Moms," cited above.

xiii **a "big problem":** Ibid.

xiii **"to earn enough to live comfortably":** Ibid.

xviii **with men who have less schooling:** Stephanie Chen, "Education, In-come, and Relationships," CNN Living, May 17, 2010, http://www .cnn.com/2010/LIVING/05/17/professional.women.date.blue.collar/. This fact was based on a study done by Pew Research Center: Richard Fry and D'Vera Cohn, "Women, Men, and the New Economics of Marriage," Pew Research Social & Demographic Trends, January 19, 2010, http://www.pewsocialtrends.org/2010/01/19/women-men-and -the-new-economics-of-marriage/.

xix **"the emotional landscapes of such families are somewhat of a mys-tery":** Hanna Rosin, "I Ain't Sayin' He's a Gold Digger," *Slate*, September 11, 2012, http://www.slate.com/articles/double_x/doublex/2012/09/ breadwinner_wives_when_the_women_make_more_money_who_ holds_the_power_.html.

xx **perform more housework and child care than their men:** Amy Tennery, "More Women Are in the Workforce—So Why Are They Still Doing So Many Chores?" *Time* (Business & Money), June 28, 2012, http://business.time.com/2012/06/28/more-women-are-in-the -workforce-so-why-are-we-still-doing-so-many-chores/.

xxi **At the end of 2012, stunning results:** Marianne Bertrand, Emir Kamenica, and Jessica Pan, "Gender Identity and Relative Income within Households," University of Chicago Booth School of Business, October 2013, http://faculty.chicagobooth.edu/emir.kamenica/docu ments/identity.pdf. Note that while the paper was published in 2013, its results started to leak at the end of 2012.

xxii **"That's bad news for the economy":** C.O., "When Women Dare to Outearn Men," *The Economist*, December 18, 2012, http://www.economist .com/blogs/freeexchange/2012/12/gender-roles.

Chapter 1

2 **to get divorced:** Derek Thompson, "A Marriage Mystery: Why Aren't More Wives Outearning Their Husbands?" *The Atlantic*, May 20, 2013, http://www.theatlantic.com/business archive/2013/05/a-marriage -mystery-why-arent-more-wives-outearning-their-husbands/276040/. See also: Adam Looney and Michael Greenstone, "The Marriage Gap," Hamilton Project, February 2012, http://www.hamiltonproject.org/ papers/the_marriage_gap_the_impact_of_economic_and_techno logical_change_on_ma/.

2 **A 2010 Cornell University study:** American Sociological Association, "Men More Likely to Cheat If They Are Economically Dependent on Their Female Partners, Study Finds," *ScienceDaily*, August 18, 2010, http://www.sciencedaily.com/releases/2010/08/100816095617 .htm. The study, "The Effect of Relative Income Disparity on Infidelity for Men and Women," was led by Christin L. Munsch.

3 **whether we choose to stay married:** In addition to the study cited in the introduction, see also Richard H. Thaler's article for the *New York Times*, "Breadwinning Wives and Nervous Husbands," June 1, 2013,

http://www.nytimes.com/2013/06/02/business/breadwinner-wives
-and-nervous-husbands.html?_r=1&.

3 **number of young married adults decreased by 30 to 50 percent:**
David Autor, "U.S. Labor Market Challenges over the Long Term,"
MIT Department of Economics and NBER, October 5, 2010, http://
economics.mit.edu/files/6341.

4 **"Our analysis of the time use data suggests":** Marianne Bertrand,
Emir Kamenica, and Jessica Pan, "Gender Identity and Relative Income within Households," University of Chicago Booth School of
Business, October 2013, http://faculty.chicagobooth.edu/emir.kamen
ica/documents/identity.pdf.

4 **still do at least two-thirds of the housework:** "How Career Women
Still Do Most of the Chores . . . Even When They're the Main Breadwinner," *Daily Mail* (UK), July 21, 2013, http://www.dailymail.co.uk/news/
article-2372772/Career-women-chores—theyre-main-breadwinner
.html. Although the study, done by Britain's Economic and Social Research Council (ESRC), looked at European households, my guess is the
numbers would reflect other households in developed nations, the
United States included.

5 **Millennial women are very close to closing the gender pay gap:** See
"On Pay Gap, Millennial Women Near Party—For Now," Pew Research
Social & Demographic Trends, December 11, 2013, http://www.pew
socialtrends.org/2013/12/11/on-pay-gap-millennial-women-near
-parity-for-now.

5 **earning about 60 percent of bachelor's degrees:** Anne Fisher, "Boys
vs. Girls: What's Behind the College Grad Gender Gap?" CNN Money,
March 27, 2013, http://management.fortune.cnn.com/2013/03/27/
college-graduation-gender-salaries/. See also: http://www.pewsocial
trends.org/2013/12/11/on-pay-gap-millennial-women-near-parity
-for-now/.

5 **The manufacturing sector has lost almost six million jobs:** Hanna
Rosin, "Who Wears the Pants in This Economy?" *New York Times*,
August 30, 2012, http://www.nytimes.com/2012/09/02/magazine/

who-wears-the-pants-in-this-economy.html?partner=rss&emc=rss
&utm_source=buffer&buffer_share=d25ed.

5 **twelve are ruled mostly by women:** Ibid.

5 **according to Pew Research Center:** Wendy Wang, Kim Parker, and
Paul Taylor, "Breadwinner Moms," Pew Research Social & Demographic Trends, May 29, 2013, http://www.pewsocialtrends.org/2013/
05/29/breadwinner-moms/.

5 **the "genderational gap":** See the "Women Moving Millions" fact sheet
at http://www.womenmovingmillions.org/how-we-do-it/facts/. Also
see the Russell Sage Foundation's book titled *The Rise of Women: Seven
Charts Showing Women's Rapid Gains in Educational Achievement*, February 21, 2013, http://www.russellsage.org/blog/rise-women-seven
-charts-showing-womens-rapid-gains-educational-achievement.

6 **"very important" that a man be ready to support a family:** "The
Decline of Marriage and Rise of New Families," Pew Research Social
& Demographic Trends, November 18, 2010, http://www.pewsocial
trends.org/2010/11/18/the-decline-of-marriage-and-rise-of-new
-families/.

6 **According to Lamar Pierce:** Bill Briggs, "For Richer or Poorer? When
Wives Make More, Some Men's Health Suffers," NBC News (Health),
May 28, 2013, http://www.nbcnews.com/health/richer-or-poorer-when
-wives-make-more-some-mens-health-6C10106852.

7 **to combat erectile dysfunction (ED), insomnia, and anxiety:** Lamar
Pierce, Michael S. Dahl, and Jimmi Nielsen, "In Sickness and In
Wealth: Psychological and Sexual Costs of Income Comparison in
Marriage," *Personality and Social Psychology Bulletin*, February 3,
2013, doi: 10.1177/0146167212475321, http://psp.sagepub.com/content/
early/2013/02/02/0146167212475321.abstract.

7 **"the social construct of marriage plays a critical role in how men
view wage comparison":** Ibid. See also Tom Jacob's article for *Pacific
Standard* and republished by *Salon*, "Study: Earning Less Than Your
Wife Is Bad for Your Libido," February 6, 2013, http://www.salon

.com/2013/02/06/earning_less_than_your_wife_can_be_bad_for_
the_ego_partner/.

7 **we're not as happy today:** Betsey Stevenson and Justin Wolfers, "The
Paradox of Declining Female Happiness," The National Bureau of
Economic Research (NBER), NBER Working Paper No. 14969, Issued
in May 2009, http://www.nber.org/papers/w14969. Also see Liza
Mundy's "The Gay Guide to Wedded Bliss," *The Atlantic*, June 2013,
http://www.theatlantic.com/magazine/archive/2013/06/the-gay
-guide-to-wedded-bliss/309317/.

8 **"It wasn't the agreement we made when we married":** Nancy Miller,
"Women as Breadwinners: Are We Still Wrestling with Roles in 2013?"
Women & Co., January 28, 2013, https://www.womenandco.com/arti
cle/women-as-breadwinners-are-we-still-wrestling-with-roles-in
-2013.jsp.

8 **married men who do traditional male chores:** Sabino Kornrich, Ju-
lie Brines, and Katrina Leupp, "Egalitarianism, Housework, and Sexual Frequency in Marriage," *American Sociological Review*, February
2013, vol. 78, no. 1, pp. 26–50, http://asr.sagepub.com/content/78/1/26
.abstract.

8 **marital satisfaction is linked to our spouse's participation in the
household:** Ibid.

16 **the highest of any income split:** Scott Behson, "Why Two-Income
Families Are Happier Than Single Earner Households," *Good Men
Project*, February 25, 2013, http://goodmenproject.com/families/why
-two-income-families-get-divorced-less-than-single-earner-househo
lds/#!ppo4j. Also see the work and research of Sharon Meers and Joanna Strober at http://www.gettingto5050.com.

19 **prefer divorce and raising their kids alone:** Kathleen Gerson, *The
Unfinished Revolution* (New York: Oxford University Press, 2011).

21 **how smart decisions get made in business:** "The Management Tip:
Tips on Decision Making," *Harvard Business Review*, http://hbr.org/
web/management-tip/tips-on-decision-making.

Chapter 2

27 **"Why Women Still Can't Have It All"**: Anne-Marie Slaughter, "Why Women Still Can't Have It All," *The Atlantic*, June13, 2012, http://www .theatlantic.com/magazine/archive/2012/07/why-women-still-cant -have-it-all/309020/.

28 **"put your foot on that gas pedal and keep it there"**: Sheryl Sandberg, *Lean In: Women, Work, and the Will to Lead* (New York: Knopf, 2013).

28 **how Gloria Steinem remarked on Sandberg's advice**: Sheelah Kolhatkar, "Alpha Dads: Men Get Serious about Work-Life Balance," *Bloomberg Businessweek*, May 30, 2013, http://www.businessweek .com/articles/2013-05-30/alpha-dads-men-get-serious-about-work -life-balance.

29 **sacrifice time with his family to pursue more money**: Ibid.

30 **face the same challenges that women do**: Michael S. Kimmel, "Why Men Should Support Gender Equity," Department of Sociology, State University of New York at Stony Brook, http://www.lehman.edu/aca demics/inter/women-studies/documents/why-men.pdf.

30 **difficult to balance work and family**: Kim Parker and Wendy Wang, "Modern Parenthood," Pew Research Social & Demographic Trends, March 14, 2013, http://www.pewsocialtrends.org/2013/03/14/modern -parenthood-roles-of-moms-and-dads-converge-as-they-balance-work -and-family/.

30 **men in dual-income households admit to experiencing work-life conflict**: Ellen Galinsky, Kerstin Aumann, and James T. Bond, "Times Are Changing: Gender and Generation at Work and at Home," Families and Work Institute 2008 National Study of the Changing Workforce (revised August 2011), http://familiesandwork.org/site/research /reports/Times_Are_Changing.pdf.

30 **a "strong, loving marriage"**: Peggy Drexler, "Citi and LinkedIn Today Released the Results from the Third *Today's Professional Women Report*," *Forbes*, October 30, 2013, http://www.forbes.com/sites/peggy

drexler/2013/10/30/citi-and-linkedin-today-released-the-results
-from-the-third-annual-todays-professional-women-report/.

31 **men spend three times as much time with their children:** Sheelah
Kolhatkar, "Alpha Dads: Men Get Serious about Work-Life Balance,"
Bloomberg Businessweek, May 30, 2013, http://www.businessweek
.com/articles/2013-05-30/alpha-dads-men-get-serious-about-work
-life-balance.

33 **"Let them try to sell that":** Stephen Marche, "Home Economics: The
Link Between Work-Life Balance and Income Equality," *The Atlantic*,
July/August 2013, http://www.theatlantic.com/magazine/archive/
2013/07/the-masculine-mystique/309401/.

35 **a blow to their self-esteem:** Katie McDonough, "Study: Men Secretly
Feel Terrible When the Women They Love Succeed," *Salon*, August 30,
2013, http://www.salon.com/2013/08/30/study_men_secretly_feel_
terrible_when_the_women_they_love_succeed/. The study was done
by Kate A. Ratliff and Shigehiro Oishi, "Gender Difference in Implicit
Self-Esteem Following a Romantic Partner's Success or Failure," *Journal of Personality and Social Psychology*, 2013, vol. 105, no. 4, pp. 688–
702, http://www.apa.org/pubs/journals/releases/psp-a0033769.pdf.

35 **the modern "hookup culture":** Katie Taylor, "Sex on Campus: She
Can Play That Game, Too," *New York Times*, July 12, 2013, http://www
.nytimes.com/2013/07/14/fashion/sex-on-campus-she-can-play-that
-game-too.html.

36 **"concentration of men who are worthy of you":** Susan A. Patton,
"Advice for the Young Women of Princeton," Opinion: Letter to the
Editor, March 29, 2013, http://thedailyprincetonian.wordpress.com
/2013/03/29/opinion-letter-to-the-editor-march-29-2013/.

38 **"10-year marriage contract":** Emma Johnson, "A 10-Year Contract
Will Save Marriage," posted May 1, 2013 on her blog at http://www
.wealthysinglemommy.com/a-10-year-contract-will-save-marriage/.

40 **women who remain childless:** Melanie Notkin, "The Truth About
the Childless Life," posted on the *Huffington Post* August 1, 2013,

http://www.huffingtonpost.com/melanie-notkin/the-truth-about-the
-childless-life_b_3691069.html.

41 **"suffer the prejudice of being an 'older' woman":** Ibid.

44 **"We were caught by surprise":** Sheryl Sandberg, *Lean In: Women,
Work, and the Will to Lead* (New York: Knopf, 2013).

46 **"By the time the third year hit":** Ralph Gardner Jr., "Alpha Women,
Beta Men," *New York*, http://nymag.com/nymetro/news/features/n_9495/.

47 **"the truth may chase their man away":** The quotes from Brad Klontz
came from a personal interview. For more on this topic, see Kimberly
Gedeon's "He's Got a Weak Ego . . . Study Finds Your Success Often Makes
Your Man Feel Like a Failure," *Madame Noire*, August 29, 2013, http://
madamenoire.com/296737/men-intimidated-by-successful-women/.

Chapter 3

55 **the woman is *twice* as likely:** "Women Call the Shots at Home; Public
Mixed on Gender Roles in Jobs," Pew Research Social & Demographic
Trends, September 25, 2008, http://www.pewsocialtrends.org/2008/09
/25/women-call-the-shots-at-home-public-mixed-on-gender-roles
-in-jobs/.

75 **"may become secretly angry":** Harriet Pappenheim and Ginny
Graves, *For Richer or Poorer: Keeping Your Marriage Happy When
She's Making More Money* (New York: Harper, 2006).

Chapter 4

83 **the number of prenups had jumped 73 percent:** Mellody Hobson,
"Why a Prenup May Be Right for You," CBS Money Watch, May 29, 2013,
http://www.cbsnews.com/news/why-a-prenup-may-be-right-for-you/.

84 **an increase in mothers paying child support:** Patricia Reaney, "Divorce Courts Mirror Society as More Women Pay Alimony," Reuters,

May 10, 2012, http://www.reuters.com/article/2012/05/10/us-divorce
-women-alimony-idUSBRE8490YW20120510.

84 **the number of women paying alimony:** Ibid.

85 **"men lose *a lot* in a divorce":** Vicki Larson, "Why Women Walk Out More Than Men," *Huffington Post*, January 24, 2011, http://www.huffingtonpost.com/vicki-larson/why-women-want-out-more-t_b_792133.html.

85 **The Marriage Project study:** For more up-to-date data about the National Marriage Project, go to the website at http://nationalmarriage project.org/.

Chapter 5

102 **Relationship coach Alison Armstrong:** To learn more about Armstrong's programs and workshops, visit her site at www.understand men.com.

103 **we women have inherited an adversarial relationship:** Ibid.

108 **"come home and suck his dick":** Ralph Gardner Jr., "Alpha Women, Beta Men," *New York*, http://nymag.com/nymetro/news/features/n_9495/.

115 **writes one blogger who makes twice what her man does:** "I Make More Money Than My Partner; Is That Emasculating?" Posted on the *XO Jane* blog, January 9, 2013, http://www.xojane.com/relationships /i-make-more-money-than-my-partner-is-that-emasculating.

116 **"has lost none of its attractions":** "Why Women Want to Marry Richer Men," *Deccan Herald*, January 4, 2013, http://www.deccanherald.com/ content/126167/content/216115/india-may-see-jobs-boom.html.

Chapter 6

119 **stuck doing the worst kind of housework:** Erin Anderssen, "Dirty Work: How Household Chores Push Families to the Brink," *Globe and Mail*, June 1, 2013, http://www.theglobeandmail.com/life/relationships/

dirty-work-how-household-chores-push-families-to-the-brink/article
12300024/?page=all.

120 **In a study of thirty-two countries:** Ibid. Also see a report from the
Canadian Labour Congress, "Women in the Workforce: Still a Long
Way from Equality," http://www.canadianlabour.ca/sites/default/files/
pdfs/womensequalityreportEn.pdf.

120 **reduced the odds that a young couple would report equal sharing:**
Anderssen, "Dirty Work."

120 **women's salaries often pay for "women's work":** Ibid.

120 **an eighty-year transformation:** Man Yee Kan, Oriel Sullivan, and
Jonathan Gershuny, "Gender Convergence in Domestic Work: Dis-
cerning the Effects of Interactional and Institutional Barriers in Large-
Scale Data," Department of Sociology, University of Oxford, Sociology
Working Papers, Paper Number 2010-03, http://www.sociology.ox.ac
.uk/materials/papers/2010-03.pdf.

121 **by covering traditional wifely roles at home:** Harriet Pappenheim
and Ginny Graves, *For Richer or Poorer: Keeping Your Marriage Happy
When She's Making More Money* (New York: Harper, 2006).

121 **As many sociologists and economists have noted from a broader
standpoint:** Anderssen, "Dirty Work."

121 **different choices about her career:** To read more about Dr. Becker's
lifetime work and download various articles and research papers, go
to his website at http://home.uchicago.edu/~gbecker/.

122 **"Housework Is an Academic Issue":** Londa Schiebinger and Shan-
non K. Gilmartin, "Housework Is an Academic Issue," American Association of University Professors, January–February 2010, http://www
.aaup.org/article/housework-academic-issue#.UqUeuo2kBZg.

122 **"who is most able to handle the chores":** Anderssen, "Dirty Work."

126 **living in a cluttered home can lead to considerable psychological
stress:** Elinor Ochs and Tamar Kremer-Sadlik, editors, *Fast-Forward*

Family: Home, Work, and Relationships in Middle-Class America (Berkeley: University of California Press, 2013), http://www.ucpress.edu/book.php?isbn=9780520273986.

126 **"We have to relinquish control":** Anderssen, "Dirty Work."

129 **"the number one most impactful change":** Gretchen Rubin, *The Happiness Project: Or, Why I Spent a Year Trying to Sing in the Morning, Clean My Closets, Fight Right, Read Aristotle, and Generally Have More Fun* (New York: Harper, 2011).

130 **better productivity and stronger skills at sticking with a budget:** Charles Duhigg, *The Power of Habit: Why We Do What We Do in Business and in Life* (New York: Random House, 2012).

131 **"shared parenting is not focused too heavily on equal housework":** Marc and Amy Vachon, *Equally Shared Parenting: Rewriting the Rules for a New Generation of Parents* (New York: Perigee, 2011).

132 **"spend about the same amount of time doing so":** Lisa Belkin, "Shared (Not Divided) Parenting," *New York Times, Motherlode* (blog), January 25, 2010, http://parenting.blogs.nytimes.com/2010/01/25/shared-not-divided-parenting/?_r=0.

132 **"how to make their joint plan actually work":** Ibid.

133 **"Fairly sharing the chores becomes a result of this mentality":** For more about the Vachons' ideas, go to www.equallysharedparenting.com.

134 **even if it's not fifty-fifty:** "Modern Marriage," Pew Research Social & Demographic Trends, July 18, 2007, http://www.pewsocialtrends.org/2007/07/18/modern-marriage/.

140 **"must hammer out every last detail of domestic life":** Liza Mundy, "The Gay Guide to Wedded Bliss," *The Atlantic*, June 2013, http://www.theatlantic.com/magazine/archive/2013/06/the-gay-guide-to-wedded-bliss/309317/.

Chapter 7

144 **experiencing more stress-related symptoms:** "Stress in America: Our Health at Risk," American Psychological Association, January 2012, http://www.apa.org/news/press/releases/stress/2011/final-2011 .pdf.

145 **"my whole family is fucked":** Hanna Rosin, "I Ain't Sayin' He's a Gold Digger," *Slate*, September 11, 2012, http://www.slate.com/articles/ double_x/doublex/2012/09/breadwinner_wives_when_the_women_ make_more_money_who_holds_the_power_.2.html.

146 **she will likely lose to that same guy:** Curt Rice, "The Motherhood Penalty: It's Not Children That Slow Mothers Down," December 8, 2011, http://curt-rice.com/2011/12/08/the-motherhood-penalty-its -not-children-that-slow-mothers-down/.

151 **we shouldn't forget to act like ladies:** "Do Women Need to Act Like Men to Be Successful Managers"? Posted on the *Naturejobs* blog by Rachel Bowden, June 24, 2011, http://blogs.nature.com/naturejobs/ 2011/06/24/do-women-need-to-act-like-men-to-be-successful -managers.

154 **"The darkest side of gossip":** Peggy Drexler, "Navigating the Perils of Office Gossip," *Psychology Today*, April 8, 2013, http://www.psycholo gytoday.com/blog/our-gender-ourselves/201304/navigating-the -perils-office-gossip.

154 **they can fulfill 60 percent of the job duties:** Georges Desvaux, Sandrine Devillard-Hoellinger, and Mary C. Meaney, "A Business Case for Women," *McKinsey Quarterly*, September 2008, http://www.womens colleges.org/files/pdfs/BusinessCaseforWomen.pdf.

157 **women who went MIA in the boardroom:** Judith Warner, "The Opt-Out Generation Wants Back In," *New York Times*, August 7, 2013, http:// www.nytimes.com/2013/08/11/magazine/the-opt-out-generation -wants-back-in.html.

159 **"she has fallen behind":** Sheryl Sandberg, *Lean In: Women, Work, and the Will to Lead* (New York: Knopf, 2013).

160 **"stay-at-home spouses has climbed nearly tenfold since 1980":** Jodi
Kantor and Jessica Silver-Greenberg, "Wall-Street Mothers, Stay-Home
Fathers," *New York Times*, December 7, 2013, http://www.nytimes
.com/2013/12/08/us/wall-street-mothers-stay-home-fathers.html?hpw
&rref=us.

165 **disproportionately feel stress related to their families' well-being:**
For more about the center's research (and to access all studies) as part
of the National Council for Research on Women, go to the website at
http://www.ncrw.org/member-organizations/center-work-life
-policy.

166 **and even premature death:** "How Much Sleep Do Adults Need?" National Sleep Foundation white paper, http://www.sleepfoundation
.org/article/white-papers/how-much-sleep-do-adults-need.

Chapter 8

171 **68 percent of married mothers with children under the age of eighteen work:** Kim Parker and Wendy Wang, "Modern Motherhood,"
Pew Research Social & Demographic Trends, March 14, 2013, http://
www.pewsocialtrends.org/2013/03/14/modern-parenthood-roles-of
-moms-and-dads-converge-as-they-balance-work-and-family/.

176 **"women's average annual earnings decrease by 20 percent":** Sheryl
Sandberg, *Lean In: Women, Work, and the Will to Lead* (New York:
Knopf, 2013).

185 **not among the 178 countries that guarantee paid maternity leave:**
Amanda Peterson Beadle, "How the Zero Weeks of Paid Maternity
Leave in the U.S. Compare Globally," Think Progress Organization,
May 24, 2012, http://thinkprogress.org/health/2012/05/24/489973/
paid-maternity-leave-us/.

185 **according to the benefits consulting firm Aon Hewitt:** Jen Wieczner,
"Why Dads Pass on Paid Paternity Leave," *Wall Street Journal*, May 12,
2013, http://www.marketwatch.com/story/88-of-dads-pass-on-paid
-paternity-leave-2013-05-09.

185 **"henpecked by their wives":** Lauren Weber, "Why Dads Don't Take Paternity Leave," *Wall Street Journal*, June 12, 2013, http://online.wsj.com /news/articles/SB10001424127887324049504578541633708283670.

190 **"Done is better than perfect":** This old maxim has gained popularity recently since it's been reported to be a statement decorating a wall in the Facebook headquarters and enjoyed by Sheryl Sandberg.

190 **"leaves parents and kids feeling discouraged":** For more about Amy McCready's ideas, go to www.positiveparentingsolutions.com.

191 **fathers in the Silicon Valley who take on a much larger role:** April Dembosky, "The Rise of Silicon Dad," *Financial Times*, April 19, 2013, http://www.ft.com/cms/s/2/885e1d28-a7c0-11e2-9fbe-00144feabdc0 .html#axzz2kHnk3x4C.

193 **moms were the biggest financial influence growing up:** Connie Prater, "Poll: Mom Matters Most in Shaping Our Financial Habits," CreditCards.com, http://www.creditcards.com/credit-card-news/mom -influences-money-management-financial-habits-1276.php.

194 **being a good parent is one of the most important things:** Eileen Patten and Kim Parker, "A Gender Reversal on Career Aspirations," Pew Social & Demographics Trends, 2012, http://www.pewsocialtrends .org/files/2012/04/Women-in-the-Workplace.pdf.

196 **some 43 percent of working women have no life insurance:** To access a library of data on women, go to Women Moving Millions at http://www.womenmovingmillions.org/how-we-do-it/facts/.

196 **meet 34 percent of that savings goal through a 529 plan:** See Fidelity Investment's "7th Annual College Savings Indicator Executive Summary of Key Findings," 2013, https://www.fidelity.com/static/dcle/welcome/documents/2013-CSI-Executive-Summary.pdf. Also see Linda DiProperzio's "How to Get a Savings Plan in Place for Baby's Future," Parents.com, 2012, http://www.parents.com/baby/care/american-baby -how-tos/baby-savings-plan/.

200 **"sometimes perceived as freeloaders":** Carol Hymowitz, "Behind Every Great Woman," *Bloomberg Businessweek*, January 4, 2012, http://www

.businessweek.com/magazine/behind-every-great-woman-01042012
.html.

Chapter 9

206 **"looking like a 'gigolo'"**: Katrin Bennhold, "Keeping Romance Alive in
the Age of Female Empowerment," *New York Times*, November 30, 2010,
http://www.nytimes.com/2010/12/01/world/europe/01iht-letter.html.

212 **have a game plan already in place:** Laurie Puhn, *Fight Less, Love
More: 5-Minute Conversations to Change Your Relationship without
Blowing Up or Giving In* (New York: Rodale, 2012).

Chapter 10

217 **female breadwinners specifically seek out and choose lower-earning
husbands:** Nina Bahadur, "Women Who Marry Lower-Earning Men
Don't Experience Wage Drop After Kids, Study Finds," *Huffington Post*,
July 17, 2013, http://www.huffingtonpost.com/2013/07/17/wage-gap
-women-breadwinners_n_3612112.html.

219 **why being the primary breadwinner can potentially be good for
your marriage:** These ideas were originally shared online in an article
I wrote for *Daily Worth* ("5 Marriage Benefits of Being the Breadwinner"), September 16, 2013, http://www.dailyworth.com/posts/2134
-5-marriage-benefits-of-being-the-breadwinner.

221 **successful marriages partly hinge on the mother's perception of the
father-child relationship:** Adam M. Galovan, et al., "Father Involve-
ment, Father-Child Relationship Quality, and Satisfaction with Family Work: Actor and Partner Influences on Marital Quality," *Journal of
Family Issues*, March 8, 2013, http://jfi.sagepub.com/content/early/
2013/03/07/0192513X13479948.abstract.

222 **"working as an indication of a mother's love":** Kathleen Gerson, *The
Unfinished Revolution* (New York: Oxford University Press, 2011).

223 **"funnel our energy into breaking this cycle":** Sheryl Sandberg, *Lean
In: Women, Work, and the Will to Lead* (New York: Knopf, 2013).